W9-DHM-696
WITHDRAWN

BK 643.55 P298
PATIOS, PORCHES, AND POOLS
1977 7.95 FV
3000 476811 30018
St. Louis Community College

PATIOS, PORCHES AND POOLS

First Published in the UK by
Marshall Cavendish Publications Limited
58 Old Compton Street, London W1V 5PA.

First Published in the USA, 1977

Distributed in the United States of America by
Chartwell Books Inc.
A division of Book Sales Inc.,
110 Enterprise Avenue, Secaucus, N.J. 07094, USA

0-89009-152-8

Some of this material first appeared in the publications
Golden Homes, All You can build in the garden and *Patios, Porches & Pools.*

**Printed in Great Britain by
Sir Joseph Causton & Sons Limited.**

Introduction

Do you ever dream of your own private swimming pool? A carport? A sun room? A glamorous patio and barbecue for entertaining your friends? But how could you possibly afford them? Here is the answer – with this book you can build them yourself at a fraction of the professional cost. Following the instructions carefully will make even the most inexperienced amateur into a competent handyman, capable of tackling the most exciting outdoor projects. *Patios, Porches and Pools* is a project handbook, full of ideas that are within the scope of your technical skill – and your pocket. You can increase the value of your property enormously, and enjoy the luxurious advantages of extras to be enjoyed all year around as well as in warm weather.

Contents

PATIOS, PORCHES AND POOLS

How often have you looked at the home of a friend or neighbour, and envied them the luxury of a sun room, or swimming pool?
Perhaps you would enjoy the relaxed atmosphere of outdoor entertaining, with a properly constructed barbecue patio, for those balmy, summer evening parties.
Patios, Porches & Pools will show you how to make a dream into a practical reality – from the luxury of a permanent swimming pool, to the functional attractions of a carport, plus all you need to know about other exciting projects. We even give you a guide to container gardening to make your patio or sun room more attractive. So draw up the plans and add to the value of your home.

Build an outdoor dining room—1

PROJECT 1

A patio built from brick and paving is one of the most attractive of outdoor home-improvement features. It can add greatly to the value of your home and embellish a very small garden. There are probably few things more pleasant than to sit outdoors on a fine day or evening. Moreover, meals in the open air, in a congenial setting, can add greatly to your enjoyment. This patio incorporates five built-in plant tubs, bench seating for eight people and a barbecue section for cooking outdoors.

The patio may be built to the 12ft 6in. size illustrated, or readily scaled up or down to suit a different location. It is partially walled, giving a degree of privacy, and incorporates five built-in plant tubs. Four of the tubs are slightly higher than the basic 3ft (910mm), to add interest to the wall line. Built-in seats provide comfortable seating for six people. A barbecue grill is incorporated, and a built-in charcoal store could be added.

A single-skin wall is used on one side of the structure. An open double wall is used on the other. This can be covered, fully or partially, with loose-laid patio slabs, to provide a serving area for the barbecue, or left uncovered as a shrub or flower planter. Offset openings provide a walk-through to the garden.

The patio was designed to suit the standard 9in. (450mm) bricks or blocks available anywhere, and although this was built in Redland 'Kentstone' any random patterning of your choice will suffice. The paving is Redland 'Polygon' but similarly you may choose any paving that suits your exterior home décor.

Choosing the site

When choosing the site, remember that the patio floor needs to slope about 3in. overall so that it will not collect rainwater. Even more important, your patio walls must not touch the house wall above the line of the dampcourse, or damp from the patio masonry may penetrate the house. Even if you take the paving slabs up to the house as part of your scheme, ensure that the top of the slab is at least 6in. below the house dampcourse.

On a flat plot of land, the easiest solution is to leave the width of a path between house and patio, and slope the patio floor away from the house.

If the ground slopes towards the house, you will need to excavate so that the patio site itself slopes away from the house, and leave some drainage holes in the brickwork. In areas where rainfall is average, as in Britain, these holes plus the gaps between the paving slabs will allow the water to seep away. In areas subject to heavy rain, you may need a land-drain from the rear of the site to a point well clear of the house.

If the ground slopes away from the house, there may be height enough to butt the patio walls against the house below the dampcourse—provided, that is, that the steps from house to patio do not intrude too far on to the patio floor. In this instance, of course, you slope the patio floor away from the house.

On a steeply sloping plot, you may need to excavate for part of the patio site and raise the ground level for the rest. In such a case, always excavate for at least two-thirds of the total area. This is because much of what you dig out will be useless as 'fill', and replacement material may be expensive. Any 'fill' will, in any event, need laborious tamping down to provide a stable base for the floor.

Clearing the site

First, equip yourself with a dozen pegs of 2in. x 2in. or 50mm x 50mm timber about 1ft long, sharpened at one end—these will be used at several stages of the job—a spade, a hammer and a steel tape.

Using the steel tape to measure both the distance from the house and the dimensions of your patio, drive four pegs into the ground, one at each corner of your proposed site. Now mark out with the spade an area about 3ft bigger all round than that enclosed by the pegs. Clear off all the grass and stack the turves well out of the way; you will need some of them later. Clear away all loamy topsoil and remove any tree roots since, if left, they might eventually dislodge the paving or crack the foundations.

Remove the four marker pegs and store them for later use.

Levelling the site

An apparently flat piece of land can often conceal, over a distance of just a few yards, a difference in levels of a foot or more. So the next stage is to get the site truly level—except, of course, for the 3in. slope for rainwater drainage. For this you will need some of your pegs; a builder's level either 3ft or 1 metre long; some

Plants in the built-in tubs add a gay splash of colour to the brick-and-paving patio. The use of block and random colour in the brick and paving adds texture and interest. The optional screen walls give privacy and enhance the overall appearance. A charcoal store can be built under the barbecue slab.

NELSON HARGREAVES

blocks of wood 3in. and 1½in. thick; and a straight-edge about 8ft (2.40m) long.

Mark your pegs with a thick pencil line right round them 2in. (50.8mm) from the top. This line represents ground level. Now drive three pegs into the ground at intervals along one side of your patio site (Fig.1)—one at what is to be the highest point when you have excavated; one in the middle; and one at what is to be the lowest point. Put a 1½in. block on the middle peg and a 3in. block on the peg at the proposed lowest point; these will compensate for the fall you want on the ground.

Use your straight-edge and builder's level over the three pegs to see how far 'out' the ground is. Where the ground is too high, pare it away with the spade until you can see, by driving the pegs in a bit more, that the levels are correct.

Next, work sideways across the site, using more of your pegs as you go; and then check the diagonals. Finally, use your straight-edge on the ground while you pare away any intermediate 'bumps'.

Setting out the site

Setting out foundation and wall positions is a job that needs some care. Should the layout go 'out of square' it will probably not be noticed immediately, but will show up badly when the paving stones fail to fit. (In house building, similarly, the error usually goes unnoticed until the roof turns out to have a 'ragged' bottom edge.)

For this job you will need profile boards and a home-made timber try-square. This latter is based on the principle that any triangle whose sides are in the ratio 3:4:5 *must* have a right angle in one corner. In practice, perhaps the handiest tool is a timber triangle whose outside edges measure 4½ft, 6ft and 7½ft respectively; it is big enough to check the 'square' of rooms (when laying floor tiles, for example) but small enough to store upright in the garage (see inset, Fig.2).

The profile board (Fig.2) consists of two crossbars of planed timber, each about 4ft 6in. or 1.5m long, mounted at right angles to each other on three pegs of 2in. x 2in. timber. For this project, a simple rectangle, you will need four sets.

Before you make up your profiles, you must first establish your 'building line'—the main line from which all other dimensions are measured. Measure the desired distance from the house at one corner of the patio site, and drive in a peg. Measure out the width of the patio, check that the distance from the house is the same as before, and drive in another peg. A line between the two is the building line.

To set up the profiles, a single stake is first driven into the ground about 2ft (610mm) diagonally outside the actual foundation area. This is called the 'datum' peg. As all other references—vertical and horizontal checks in laying foundations and in building walls—are

This plan view of the patio shows the arrangement of plant tubs and barbecue. The slabs on the wall alongside provide a serving facility, but are loose laid and some or all could be removed for planting shrubs and flowers.

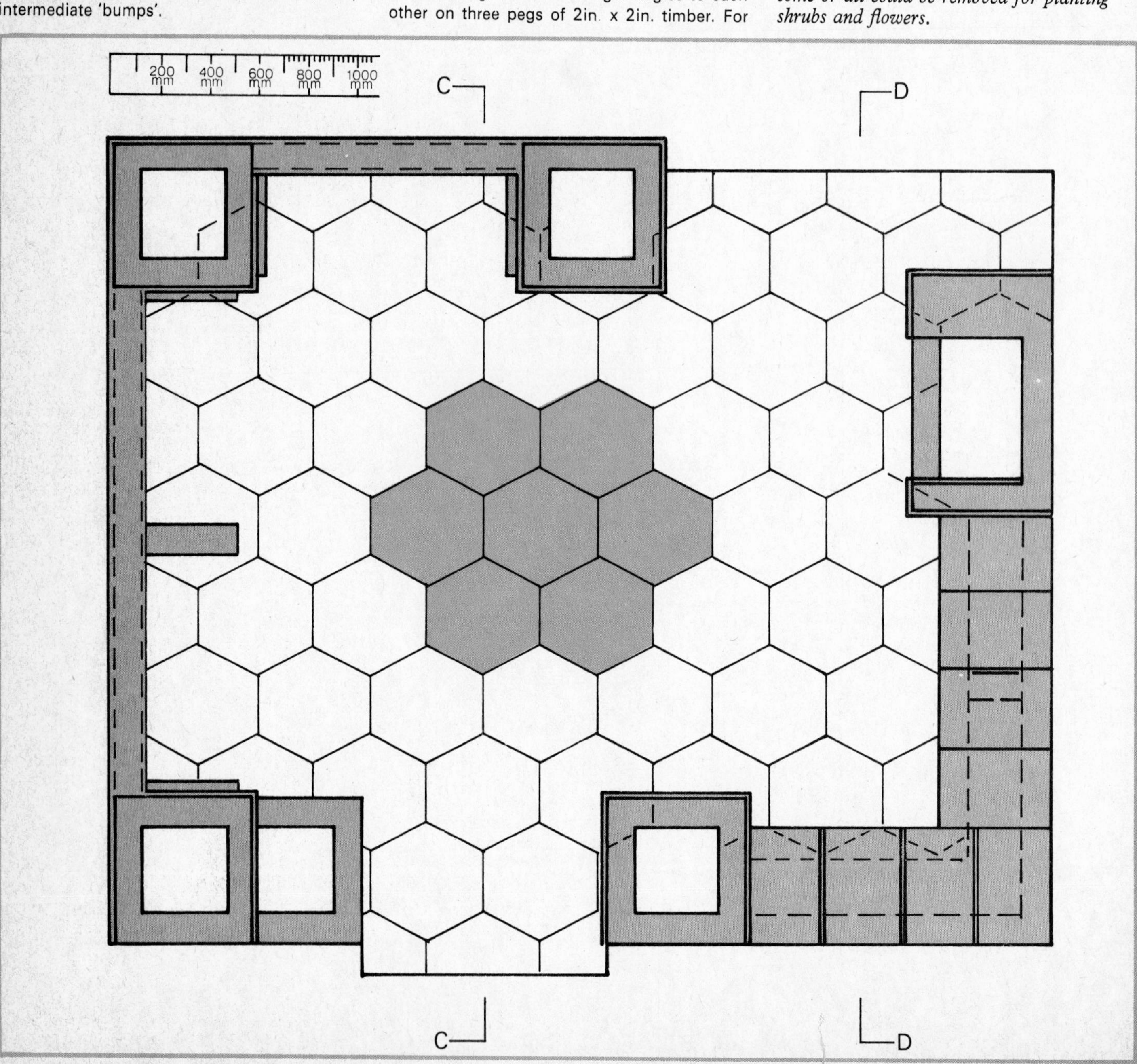

taken from this peg, it should never be disturbed. Ideally, it should be set in concrete and uprooted only when the job is over.

Next, pegs are driven in at right angles on either side of the datum peg (Fig.2) and the first profile boards are nailed to these. Each board must be exactly level along its own length, and the pair must be level with each other; use the builder's level to make sure.

Similar sets of profiles are built outside each of the other three corners. No matter how much the ground slopes, all four sets must be exactly level with one another. You can check this by using the straight-edge and builder's level; where the span is too great for the straight-edge, temporary pegs can be driven in as intermediate supports. (Since a length of timber is almost never exactly straight, even a so-called straight edge will produce some inaccuracies. To correct this, each span should be checked first with one edge up and then with the opposite edge up, and the builder's level should always be placed in the middle of the board.)

Once the profile boards have been levelled, the next job is to stretch lines across them to mark exactly where the outside edges of the brickwork will be. For this, nylon fishing line is better than string, which sags as the humidity varies.

Sight the first nylon line (marked a-b in Fig.2) across the profiles and directly above the two pegs that marked your original 'building line'; make a tiny saw cut in each profile board; and draw the line tightly between the notches, securing it with a knot at each end. Repeat the procedure for the two lines running off at right angles (a-c and b-d in the diagram), using the large wooden try-square to see that the corners are square. (You will need some help at this stage.) Again using the try-square, site the line c-d, at the opposite end.

Now check that the dimensions are correct at both ends and on both sides. Check that your levels are accurate—and not, for example, 'high' at one corner—by lying down and sighting across the lines at opposite ends. Finally, measure the diagonals a-d and b-c with a steel tape; unless the diagonals are exactly the same you are 'out of square' and must make some adjustments. When you are satisfied that your lines are true, rule vertical pencil lines down the inside of the profiles so that, after you have moved the nylon lines later, you can replace them in the correct notches.

The other line positions can now be marked quickly, and by measurement only. The outer edge of the foundations, or 'footings', should be $4\frac{1}{2}$in. (112mm) wider than the walls. Working from your existing nylon lines, measure outwards for $4\frac{1}{2}$in. all round, cut a new series of notches, and again rule vertical lines down the insides of the profiles.

This project, to save having a complicated series of footings, uses a wide 'slab' footing to run the full width of its planters and seats. The third series of lines on Fig.2 is to line up the brickwork on the inside of the planters and so on. The correct dimensions shown in the plan, on page 4 should also be measured from your first set of nylon lines, the profile boards notched and the usual vertical lines ruled.

Digging the footings

Trenches for the footings should be dug to a depth of about 9in. (222mm) so that neither footings nor bedding mortar will show above ground level. Although the patio floor is intended to slope, the walls (and hence the foundations under them) should be level. So you will need to dig deeper than 9in. as you work up the slope.

While you are digging, use only the inner and outer profile lines as a guide—any other lines will only get in the way.

Once dug, the trenches can be checked for width and alignment by using the builder's level, this time held upright against the profile lines (Fig.3). To establish the correct depth of concrete and an accurate level on which to begin bricklaying, next drive in a series of pegs so that their tops will be level with the top of the concrete; this should be about 4in. (102mm) thick. Since these pegs will finish up jammed in the concrete, use pieces of boxwood or other scrap material. Use the straight-edge and builder's level to see that the tops of the pegs are, in fact, level (Fig.4).

If the site slopes steeply, you may have to 'step' the footings to keep them out of sight below ground level. Make each step the same depth as one brick and its mortar joint, or two bricks and two joints. This is so you can begin your bricklaying on the lowest step, bringing other courses into line as you work upwards.

Pouring the concrete

A mixture of one part (by volume) of Portland cement, $2\frac{1}{2}$ parts of sand and four parts of coarse aggregate is a suitable composition for the concrete. It should be mixed fairly dry and, once poured in, well tamped to remove air pockets, mix in the water and 'hydrate' the cement. In hot weather, the mix should be covered with sacking or old cement bags and kept moist. Although concrete takes about 21 days to cure, the foundations should be firm enough for bricklaying in about a week. Avoid laying concrete in icy weather, since frost can damage it.

Now you are ready to begin bricklaying.

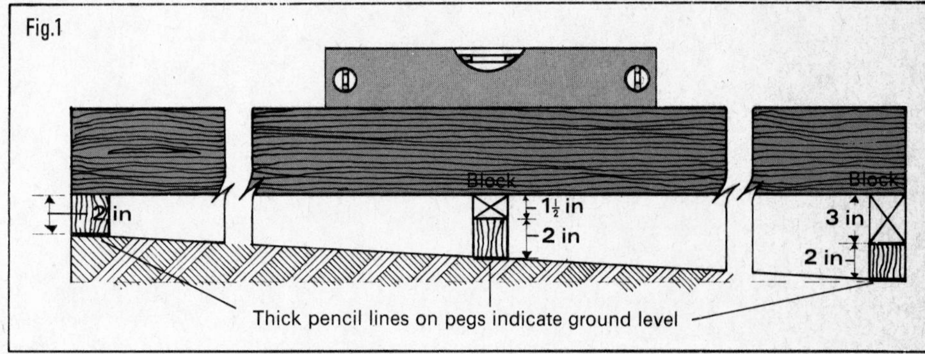

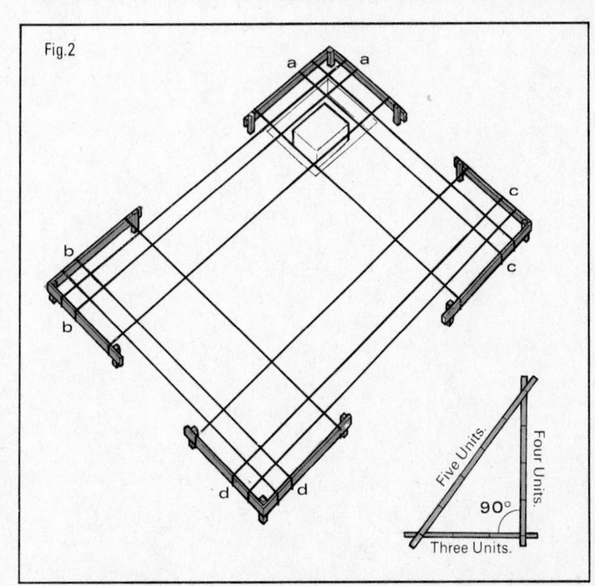

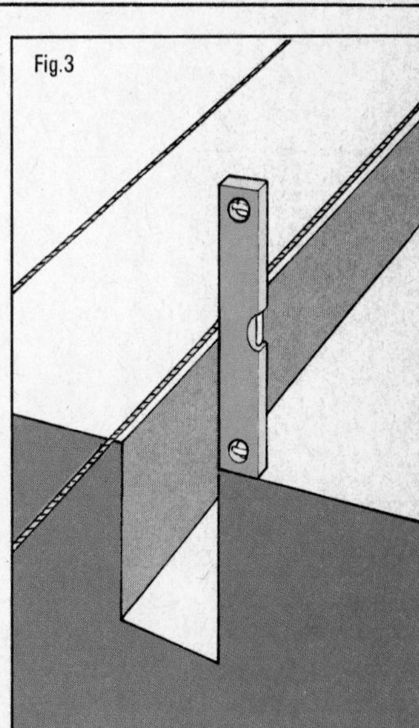

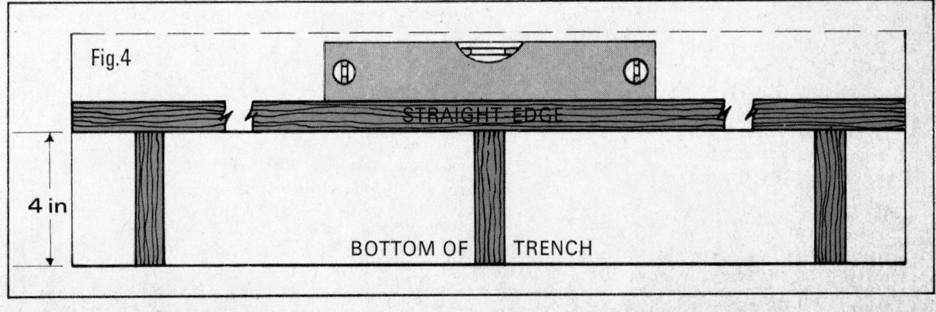

Build an outdoor dining room—2

A well-designed patio is a valuable addition to the home and also a social asset, a place to invite people to meet and to enjoy themselves.

Top right: *A barbecue is an open fire, consisting of a simple grill with a tray of burning charcoal beneath it. All manner of foods can be prepared on this out-of-doors 'kitchen range'.*

Bottom right: *This shows the layout of the seating between flower tubs. The central area enables a table as well as extra seating to be introduced.*

A patio is very much a room outdoors, an extension to the home which is best enjoyed in fine weather. It is an ideal place on which to throw a party and to serve food cooked over the barbecue grill. As a prelude to that party, this chapter shows how to complete the job and add that extra vista to your home.

Preparing for bricklaying

Once the foundations for your patio have been laid, you can set out the site ready for bricklaying.

First, you want one set of your profile strings lined up with the outside edge of the brickwork. Move them to the appropriate notches on the profile boards. At intervals of about 6ft (or 2 metres), space out 'spot' boards about 2ft (or 600mm) square, made from scrap wood, to hold supplies of mortar. Stack your bricks neatly between them. You need about 25 bricks for each square yard covered.

The tools you will need are the spirit level; the straight-edge; a 10in. or 11in. (254mm or 279mm) bricklayer's trowel; a small pointing trowel called a *dotter*; a club hammer; a wire brush; a bolster or cold chisel, for cutting bricks and paving slabs; a shovel for mixing the mortar; and a pair of bricklayer's pins with a few yards of cord.

Bricklaying mortar mix consists of one part (by volume) of cement to eight parts of sand, with one part of lime or its equivalent in proprietary plasticizer (see the instructions on the tin) to make the mixture 'fatty' and more easily workable. In cold weather, slightly less sand should be used.

Before laying the first course of bricks, spread a *bedding* course of mortar screed about 1in. (25mm) thick along the foundations. Before this has set, draw on it the 'course line' to which you lay your bricks. You do this by holding the builder's level upright, resting on the mortar and with its edge against the profile line, and scratching a trowel mark on the mortar. Do this every few feet, and then join up the marks. When you come to lay the bricks, lay them to this line, but be careful not to cover it.

Laying the bricks

Bricks can be laid either longways or endways, to give a variety of brick styles or bonds. The one used here is a *stretcher bond*; all the bricks are laid lengthwise.

In bricklaying, the ends of a wall are always built up first. Then a cord is stretched from one end to the other while the intermediate bricks are laid. This keeps each successive course level, and ensures that the top of the wall is straight.

Begin by building up your first two *quoins* (corners) at opposite ends of the patio. Form the corners by laying bricks alternately on each other at right angles. Build up to the full height by *racking back*—laying one brick less in each successive course. Remember to allow for drainage holes, where these are needed. Use the builder's level as you go to check that the bricks are level, plumb and flush. Any adjustments to the levels of the bricks are made by tapping down the bricks with the handle of the trowel, and striking off with the trowel edge any excess mortar that is squeezed out.

With the first pair of quoins built up, use a cord stretched between two bricklayer's pins to help level the intermediate bricks as you lay them. The pins are tucked into the mortar joints around each corner of the wall, with the line snagged over the top edges of a quoin brick at each end. Take up any slack in the line by winding it over the spade-shaped part of the bricklayer's pins.

Laying out a few bricks 'dry' will help you to ensure that you are spacing them correctly. Minor adjustments can be made by varying the thickness of mortar in the vertical joists. If some cutting is needed, use the bolster and club hammer, and work right round the brick with even blows. The professional will cut a brick with the edge of his bricklaying trowel, but this is a practised art.

Before you build any of the interior walls, note that the barbecue pit requires some steel insets in the brickwork, and that built-in seating, should you desire it, requires coping stone insets as supports. So check the instructions for both barbecue and seating before proceeding too far.

Pointing and coping

As each wall is built, the joints must be *pointed*, or finished, while the mortar is still fairly soft. The flush joint illustrated here is achieved by scraping horizontal joints with the edge of the bricklayer's trowel, and vertical joints with the 'dotter' trowel.

After the mortar is surface-dry (usually overnight), any surface blemishes on the bricks are removed by a light wire brushing.

Once the walls are built, the *coping* (capping) pieces are mortared in, using the same technique as for bricklaying.

NELSON HARGREAVES

Paving the patio

When buying patio slabs, allow about 5 per cent extra for breakages; however careful you are in cutting, a few will always break in the wrong place.

Paving slabs need a firm base. If the ground is soft, it is advisable to provide a foundation of well-consolidated hardcore. Where this is done, use the straight-edge, level and pegs again to see that the base is even, with the correct 'fall' for rainwater drainage.

Paving slabs should always be laid with the textured, non-slip surface upwards. Before laying begins, a few slabs should be set out, 'dry', to see where cutting will be needed. You do not want to finish with three-quarters of a slab on one side of an opening and only a quarter of a slab on the other. A nylon line stretched across the ground will help you align your first row.

The actual laying technique will vary according to the density of the sub-soil, the local weather, the amount of 'traffic' you expect on the patio, and your personal taste:

1, Where some slight settlement of the surface can be accepted, or where rainfall is sparse, a layer of finely sifted soil or sand can be spread over the area and the slabs laid, carefully but firmly, on this.

2, Where you want greater surface stability, spread sifted soil or sand as before, and lay the slabs with a trowel-full of mortar under each. Larger slabs—18in. or 457mm each, say—should have a spot of mortar under each corner. Leave the paving to set for two or three days.

3, Where the surface is to be subjected to heavy wear, and especially in sub-tropical areas subject to heavy rain, prepare a fairly stiff 1 :5 cement mortar mix and spread it evenly over the surface, covering just enough ground for one slab at a time.

Slabs should not be 'pummelled' into place to correct unevenness, but tapped gently with the base of the club hammer. Use a straight-edge as you go, to check that adjoining slabs are flush.

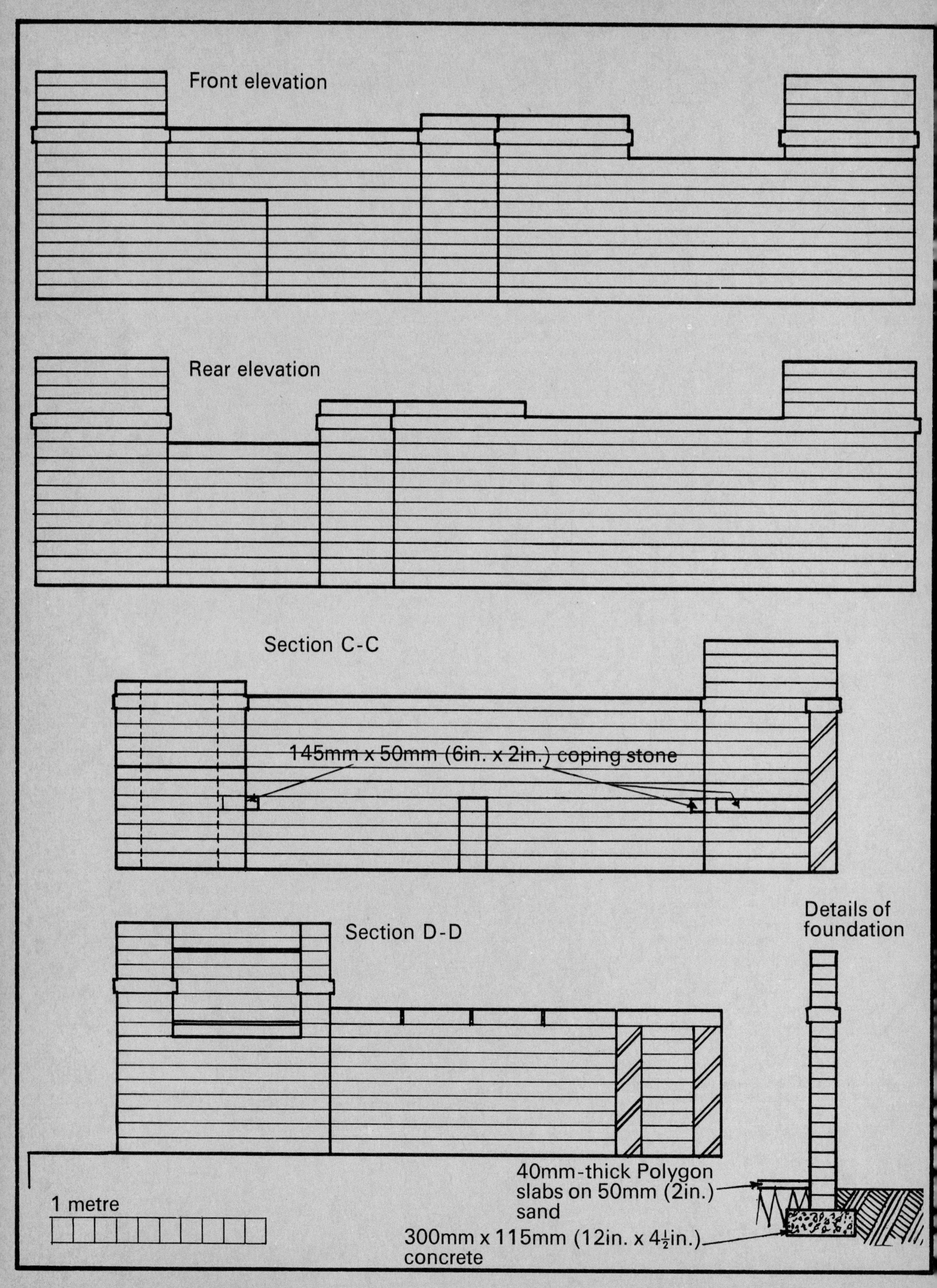
Front elevation
Rear elevation
Section C-C
145mm x 50mm (6in. x 2in.) coping stone
Section D-D
Details of foundation
40mm-thick Polygon slabs on 50mm (2in.) sand
300mm x 115mm (12in. x 4½in.) concrete
1 metre

When you need to cut a slab, first mark the cutting line with pencil and straight-edge. Now tap gently with the hammer and bolster or cold chisel to cut a shallow scratch across the face of the slab. Do the same on the back, and join the scratch lines at the edges.

Deepen the scratches by working progressively round the slab. After a while, the ringing note of the blows will deaden, indicating that the slab is cracking apart. A few more taps will make it break neatly along the line; minor irregularities can be carefully chipped off.

Once the paving has set, a dry mortar mix can be brushed into the joints. This is known as *grouting*. Be sure you leave none on the surface of the slabs; what you cannot brush away, a damp cloth will pick up.

Alternatively, the joints can be filled with finely sifted soil (you will have to keep 'topping it up' for a few weeks) and tiny plants allowed to grow.

Fitting the barbecue

The barbecue consists of an adjustable grill made of mild-steel rods and a metal tray for holding charcoal. These are mounted on angle-iron runners.

The supports for the brazier tray are made of two pieces of 2in. x 1½in. (50mm x 38mm) angle-iron. These should be 17in. (426mm) long and set 1½in. (38mm) into the mortar above the fifth brick course.

The brazier tray is made from a sheet of 22-gauge mild steel 22in. (560mm) wide—or slightly narrower if required to fit between the brickwork on either side—and 19in. (492mm) long. The front and back are bent upwards (for about 2in., and at about 45°) to retain the charcoal. Holes, 1in. (25mm) in diameter and about 4in. apart, are drilled in the bottom to provide a draught.

You need six pieces of the same size angle-iron for the grill supports. The first pair is set above the eighth course of bricks, the second above the ninth, and the third pair above the tenth course. These positions allow the grill to be set at three levels to provide different cooking temperatures for various types of food.

Ten pieces of ⅜in. (9.5mm) mild-steel rod, each one 22½in. (565mm) long, are used for the grill surface. These are welded to a U-shaped rod of the same thickness. The grill should be made so that the ends of the rods rest on the angle-iron supports, and the U-shaped rod fits between. If you do not have a welding kit, a smith or garage can do this for you.

The arrangement of the walls beside the barbecue allows for a charcoal store to be incorporated if desired. In this case a sheet of polythene (polyethylene) should be introduced beneath the coping slab. A door can be set in, using a simple framework attached to the brickwork with masonry nails.

Seating

The type of seating used is optional. Deck chairs or garden loungers, park-bench type seating or metal garden seats can be used. If built-in wooden seating is required, support it by building paving slabs into the appropriate walls, at the points shown in section CC so they project about 2in. (or 50mm). Intermediate supports in brickwork are shown in the same diagram. Before cutting and fitting the seats—they are made up as complete frames—lay a dampcourse of bituminous felt between masonry and woodwork. Ensure that nails and screws used in making the framework are of the non-rusting type.

Fig. 1 (left). The elevations show where coping stones have to be set in to provide support for permanent wooden seating.

***Top right.** The serving area alongside the barbecue is an optional feature. As an alternative, the top slabs could be left off and this area used for planters.*

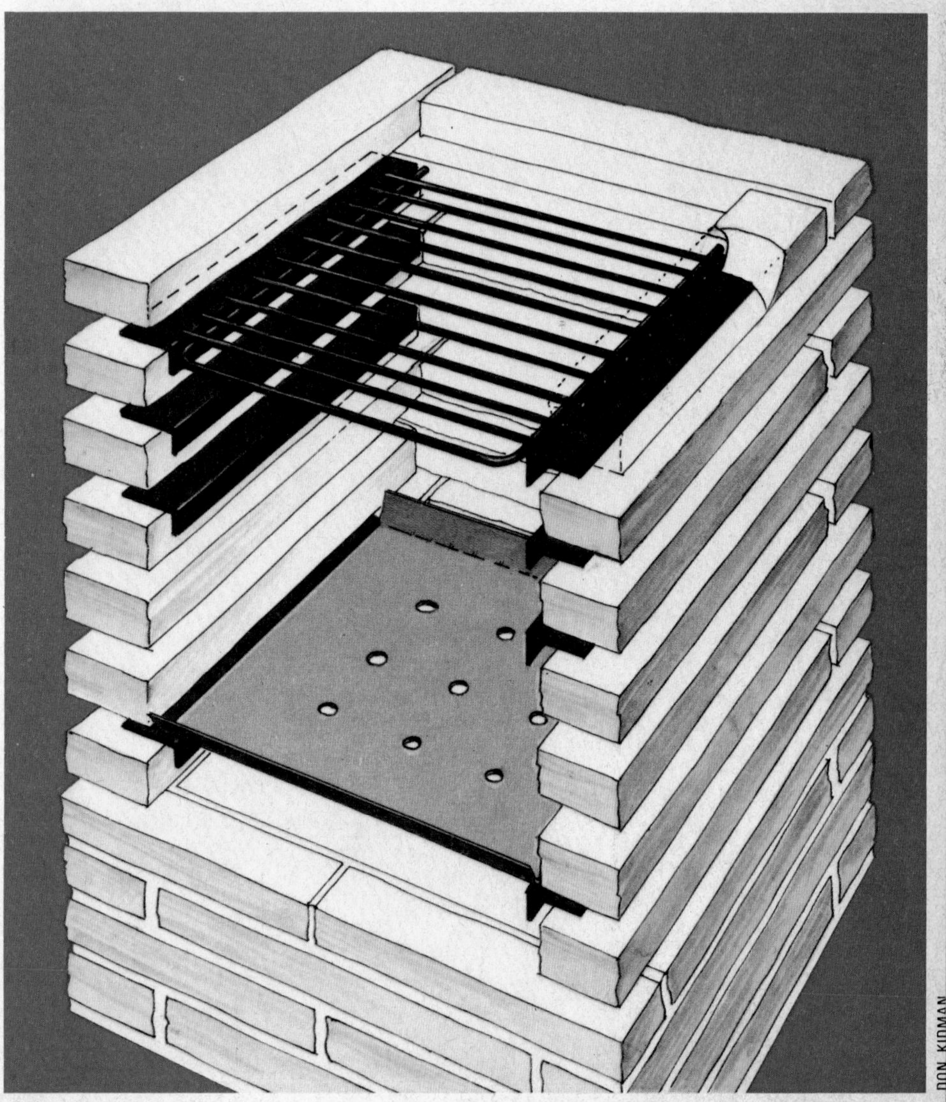

***Fig. 2** (right) The grill, made from ⅜ in. rods, can be set at three different levels to adjust the cooking temperature. The tray is of mild steel sheet.*

GAUNT
30

How to put up a carport

PROJECT 2

In many situations a carport is much better value than a garage. A garage costs more and takes longer to build, but a carport performs much the same function and can be just as attractive. If you want to provide cover for your car, a carport could be the answer.

A carport is not necessarily a cheap, unsatisfactory structure—in fact it has certain advantages over a garage. It could be constructed with the idea of providing a garage in the future; for instance you can lay a good solid foundation under a simple superstructure that can be replaced by solid walls and a door at a later date.

What is a carport?

There is no single definition of what constitutes a carport, but broadly speaking, it is a shelter that protects the car from vertical rain, but not necessarily angled rain or snow driven in by the wind. At its most elaborate, a carport could have a roof and side walls, but no doors at the front or back (see Fig.1). The simplest type would be a relatively light roof supported with struts or columns (see Fig.3).

It is important that you get a clear idea of what a carport is for the purpose of obtaining planning or building permission. The trouble is that various local authorities have slightly different opinions about the definition of a carport, so it is best to contact your own local authority before you start to draw plans. Some councils will allow carports but not garages; some rule the other way round!

Why build a carport?

Some of the reasons for building a carport —time, cost, or using it as one stage towards eventually building a garage—have been given above, but there are many more. For instance the space you have available might be wide enough to take a car, but too narrow to enable the car doors to be opened if a wall were on each side. This would make the construction of a garage impossible, but a simple carport consisting of corner columns or struts could well provide your car with some form of cover while still enabling you to open the doors.

Another point is—how often do you actually garage your car? Many people park their cars in the drive most of the time, and only garage it in the fiercest winter weather. And when you consider that a warm damp garage actually accelerates rust corrosion, such cars would actually be better off in a carport, protected from rain yet never becoming warm.

If you already have a garage that is set well back (in many cases the drive runs along the side of the house and the garage is located in or about the rear garden) then a carport built on to the side of your house would provide additional protected parking, either for a second car or when you are using the garage for other purposes, such as a workshop. And it will normally be closer to the front door—an added convenience in wet weather.

Types of carport

As mentioned, carports can range in structure from the very simple to the fairly complicated. There are also carport kits available in most countries. These are usually well worth considering, although you have not got the same flexibility that you have when doing the whole job yourself; for instance sometimes you are limited to specific dimensions.

The most simple carport is a light roof supported by metal or timber struts, as shown in Figs.2 and 3. The roof is a timber frame covered with corrugated plastic sheet or timber panelling and roofing felt. Its vertical supports are metal struts in either mild steel rod or aluminium tubing as shown in Fig.3, or sturdy timber members as in Fig.2. If the base is suitable to park a car on, you only need to dig a small hole immediately under each of the supports in the way of foundation work.

More complex carports are shown in Figs.1 and 4. The one in Fig.4 has a roof supported on one side along the house wall, and on the other side by three brick piers. The spaces between the piers at the sides can be left open or filled with plain or stone-faced ornamental bricks. The port in Fig.1 is built on the same principle, but here the piers consist of special screen walling pier blocks. The base has a brick plinth wall, and the spaces between the piers are filled with screen walling. For both these types you must have a strip foundation running underneath the walling and piers.

If your house is of timber construction, or perhaps faced with timber, you might consider a carport constructed entirely in wood. This is a much more complex stucture, however, and is outside the scope of this project.

Left. *This structure is a composite of some of the carports described here. In this case it serves as an extended porch and carport, with room for three cars. The main supports are of timber; on one side the supports are filled in between with brickwork which has four-course slots left in, mainly as a decorative feature. The opposite side has a brick plinth wall that also acts as a fence—a useful item, bearing in mind the drop below!*

DOUGLAS BAGLIN

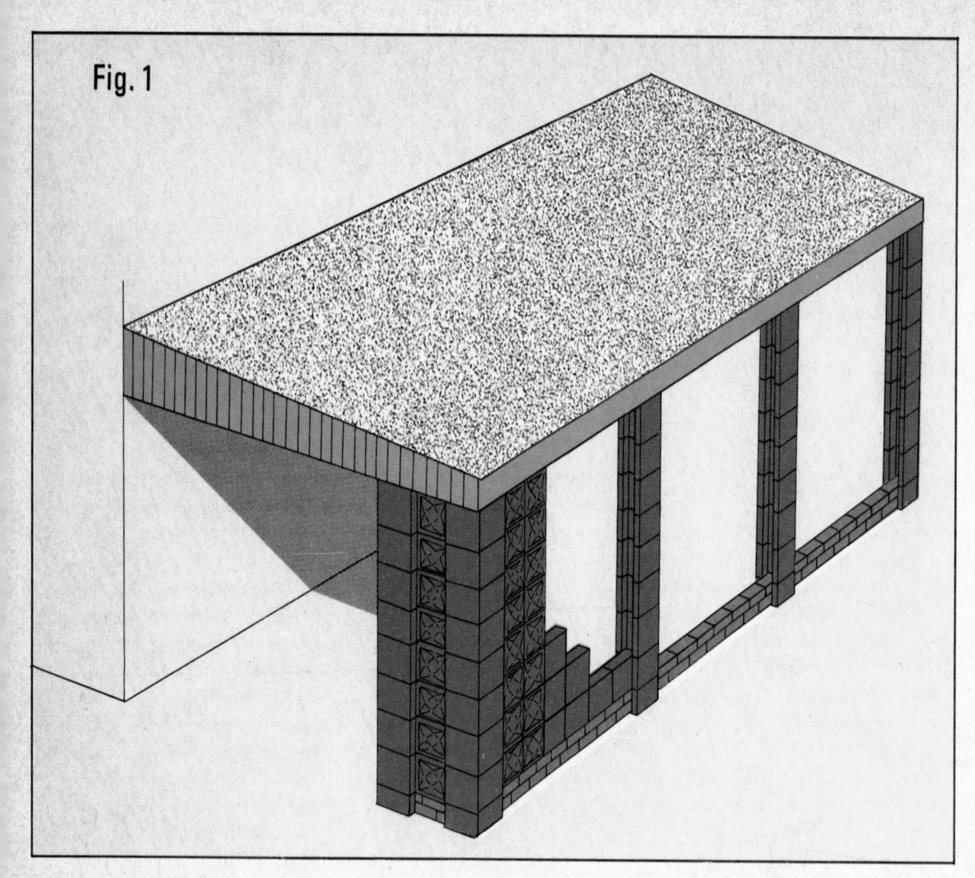

Fig.1. Screen blocks provide a very attractive walling for a carport, but the blocks themselves require strengthening if the wall is more than 3ft or 1m high. This is achieved by placing piers—which are specially made blocks—at approximately 6ft or 2m intervals, and making a short return wall at one or both of the ends.

Fig.2. Sturdy timbers provide excellent support for a light roof. The base of each timber is encased in a short brick pier, which eliminates the necessity of bedding it into the foundation concrete, where it would be permanently damp and rot away. For extra protection a window framework can be built between the supports and glazed.

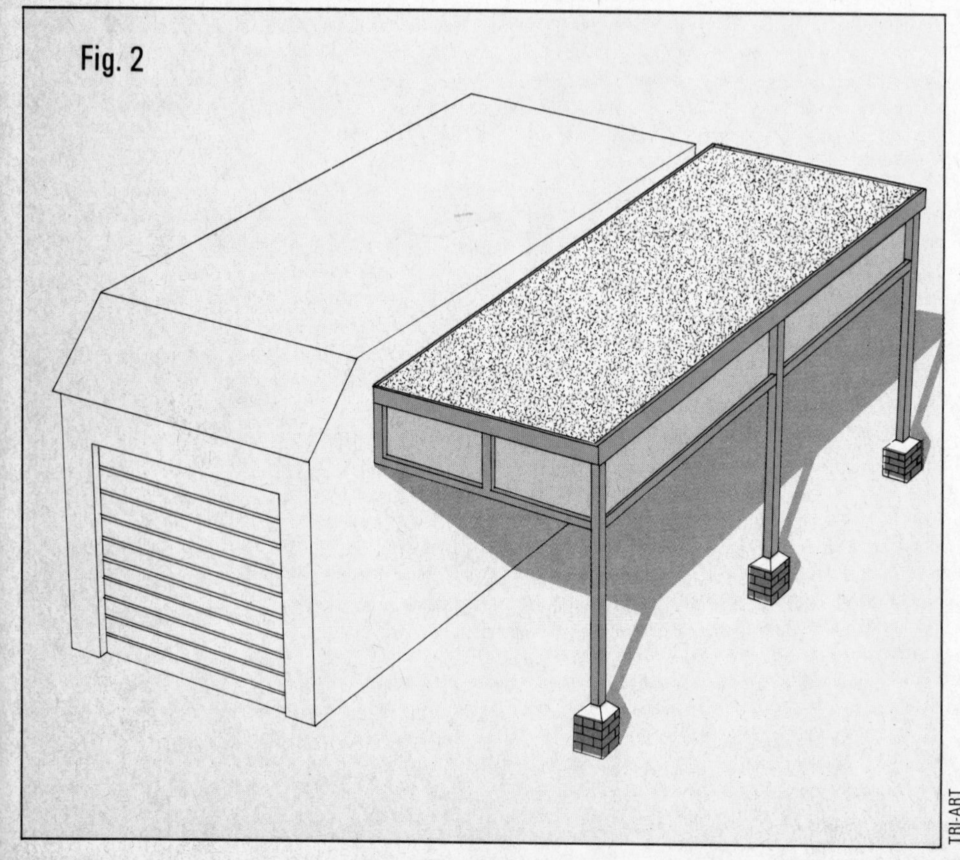

Planning and design

A carport is a relatively light form of construction, so planning or building permission is usually easily obtained for one. However this does not mean that you do not have to seek approval, because in most countries permission must be obtained for any external work that involves an extension of some sort. So submit building plans to your local authority, **to make sure you are not contravening any local bye-laws, before you start.**

When planning the actual design of the carport, bear in mind that it should harmonize **with your house in design (sketches on paper** will help you here), and that the materials and colours should also match. If you put up any old carport just for convenience or cheapness, the house and carport might make an ugly combination. For instance a carport with a roof of corrugated plastic, supported by chromium plated steel rods, would look unsightly against a Victorian house.

The base, where the car will be parked, is the first stage in planning. It may be that you only require a lightweight carport such as those shown in Figs.2 and 3, in which case the surface already in existence will probably do. A concrete or asphalt base is perfectly adequate, and even a soil base can be adequately consolidated by ramming gravel well in—though this will probably have to be repeated every year. If you are considering the heavier type of carport shown in Figs.1 and 4, then you will have to lay a suitable strip foundation; or if you want to build a garage eventually, a strip and **raft foundation. So the method you use depends on your plans for the future.**

One convenient method for a base is to lay concrete paving slabs on a 2in. or 50mm bed of well compacted sand; or two lines of slabs as wheel tracks with a centre strip of dark gravel to hide any oil drips from the car.

The choice of walls or support will depend on the degree of protection required. If you already have a garage and will use the carport as an additional convenient parking space, then simple side struts could be sufficient. On the other hand, if the carport is to be used as a permanent parking space, then you will require a greater degree of protection with side walls, something like the one in Fig.1. The aspect is also important; for example in Britain a carport that is exposed to north and east winds needs greater protection than one which faces south or west.

Building considerations

It is impossible to give detailed instructions for building a wide range of carports, but there are many points that must be mentioned here because they are not dealt with anywhere else in this publication.

If you are using struts or timber members for supporting the roof, then these must be of sufficient strength to do their job. Timber members must be at least 4in. or 100mm square; mild steel rod about 1½in. or 38mm in diameter; and aluminium support tubing about 3in. or 75mm in diameter. In each case, place the struts at about 9ft or 3m centres.

Supports do more than take a compressive strain (the weight of the roof pressing down);

they also have to stand the 'stretching' action that takes place when the wind gusts underneath the roof and tries to lift it. For this reason supports must be very securely fixed at both ends.

Metal supports can be obtained with 6in. or 150mm square base plates welded on so that they can be bedded in concrete or brickwork. If you can't obtain such supports, have plates welded on. It is easier to fit base plates on to timber members, but bear in mind that all such wood must be well soaked in creosote or a similar wood preservative, particularly the part underground where it can rot without being seen.

Brick piers as in Fig.4, whether filled in between or not, have tremendous strength, but walls and piers of lightweight screen blocks are nowhere near as strong. For this reason they must never be built in a straight run of wall. This is why the carport in Fig.1 has return corners at each end (and an extra pier) to give it maximum strength. These return corners obviously take up drive-in space and must be taken into account when planning the carport.

If the carport is to be attached to your house, there will probably be laws or regulations that limit the materials used to those that are most fire resistant. Bitumastic felted roofs, timber, glass and asbestos come well within the scope of most regulations, but some of the cheaper forms of plastic do not. So it is essential to seek the advice of your local authority to find out whether there are any materials that you are not permitted to use.

There are several different methods of butting or fixing the roof joists to the house wall. Screwing or bolting a wall plate to it is the most common, but metal 'shoes' or joist hangers, while requiring more care in setting and alignment, give a much neater finish to the job. Whatever method is used, try to avoid cutting out brickwork to receive the ends of the joists. Wood enclosed in brickwork tends to rot, and if you ever want to remove or re-site the carport you will have to make good the brickwork instead of just filling in a few bolt holes.

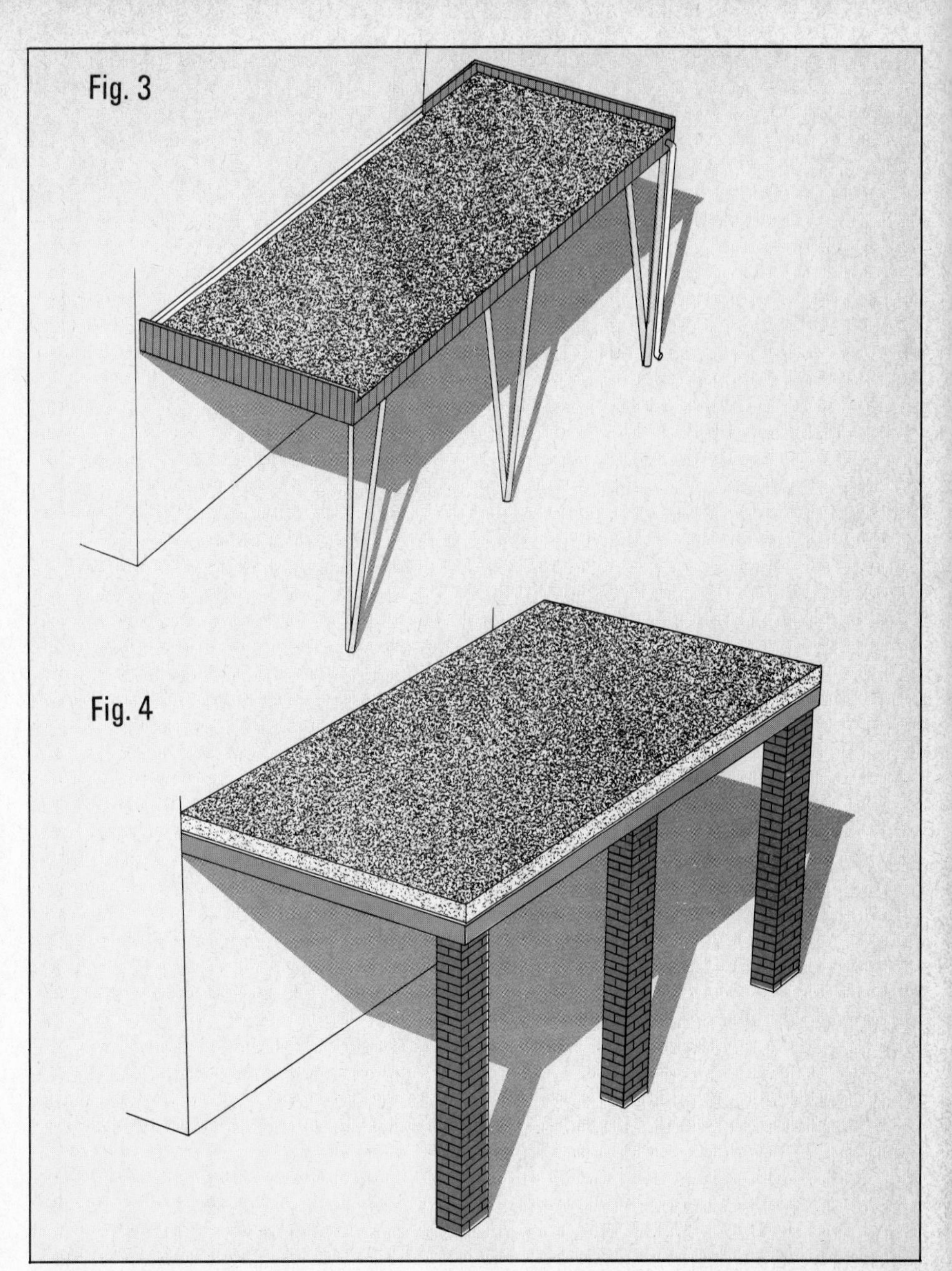

Fig.3. Metal struts are the most convenient form of support. You can use either mild steel rods or aluminium support tubing. The struts must be placed in pairs, slightly splayed as shown, with each pair at 9ft or 3m intervals. A carport like this is not only easy to construct—it is also easy to remove if you want to replace it with a more substantial garage at a later date.

***Fig.4.** Brick piers have enormous strength and are another convenient form of support; but make sure the bricks match, or at least harmonize, with the house brickwork. Piers can also provide a basis for several different designs. For instance the spaces between the piers can be filled with screen blocks, or battening can be fixed vertically on the outside of each pier and boarding such as weatherboard fixed across them.*

***Right.** If brick walls are alternated with sections of screen blocks, this will avoid a monotonous run of walling.*

DOUGLAS BAGLIN

Above. *This carport is an example of attractive simplicity. Garden walling has been used to support one side, and the other side is supported by a masonry pier of blocks of the type shown in Fig.9.*

How to put up a carport: 2

Once you have decided whether a carport or a garage will suit you best, and have come down in favour of a carport, the next step is to sit down with pencil and paper and decide on the type that will best suit your house.

The right design is important at this stage. After all you don't want the carport to *look* as though it has been added almost as an afterthought. It should, ideally, look as though it has been designed and built as part of the house. Get the most artistic member of the family, or a friend, to draw a three-quarter view of your house, (i.e. seen from the corner) at about 45 degrees on the side where the carport is to go. Then use a pencil to draw in the various carports shown here, one at a time. You should soon find the design that looks best with your house.

General construction details

Two types of carport are described here, one with metal or timber supports for the roof and the other with masonry supports, in this case brick piers or screen walling. But although the methods of support are different, the roof is Virtually identical in each, the construction conforming to the outline illustrated in Fig 8 on page 16.

The roof can be either boarded over and covered with roofing felt, or covered with translucent corrugated roofing plastic sheet. The second method is more popular because it is quicker to lay and allows in more light—particularly important if you are working on the car, or if the carport would otherwise blot out a window.

The roof joists butting against the house can be fixed in many ways, and three of the most popular—a wall plate, joist hangers and metal angle strip, are shown in Fig.1. The angle strip is not to be recommended in structures such as this, particularly if you are building a lightweight carport. The reason for this is that wind will gust into a carport and under the roof, causing a lifting effect. And as you can see in Fig.1, it is very difficult to secure joist ends to angle strip in such a way as to resist a lifting force.

Don't forget the drainage. You will have to provide some means of getting rid of rainwater. This means either running a trough or channel along the ground to an existing gulley trap, or making a soakaway. The former method entails less hard labour.

The dimensions of the structure should, ideally, be designed to accommodate at least a medium-sized car. It is no use having a space that will protect a tiny car, and then buying something much larger at a later date, and finding that it doesn't fit in. And don't forget the height. The internal height should be great enough to take a medium-sized car with a laden roof rack on top. This could easily be about 6ft or 1.8m high, so to give yourself sufficient working space the height from floor to rafters should be at least 7ft or 2m. The length of an average car, in Britain at least, is about 14ft or 4.3m, so you should aim for a carport at least 20ft or 6m in length. Some American cars are nearly 21ft (6.4m) long and will need a huge carport 26ft (8m) long.

The lightweight carport

Two types of roof support are described here, a strutted version, supported by mild steel rod or aluminium tubing, and one with vertical timbers. Both these types have an advantage over, say, masonry supports, in that they do not require extensive foundations because of their relatively light weight.

For a lightweight carport, the base requires a minimum of reconstruction. Foundation concrete will have to be laid at the base of the timbers or struts, but apart from this you can leave the base as it is unless it consists of sand or something else unsuitable for parking on. An existing concrete or asphalt surface is fine. If the base is soil, then a good layer (at least 1in. or 25mm thick) of gravel can be rolled or rammed in, but this process will have to be repeated from time to time as the car tyres scour grooves in the gravel and soil.

First (and this applies to any of the carports) mark out the outline of the carport on the ground and the walls of the house. This means drawing a line along the house wall to indicate the top level of the wall plate, or the bottom of the joist hangers, and further lines down the walls and round the base area.

Unless the base or foundation is already sufficiently strong, you will have to excavate foundation trenches in the area immediately under the struts or timbers. Excavate an area about 16in. or 400mm square, and 12in. or 300mm deep if you are using metal struts, or alternatively 9in. or 225mm deep if using timber supports.

If you already have a solid floor, this will mean chiselling out some of it; this is best done with a cold chisel and 3lb or 1.5 kg club hammer.

When this has been done, fill the trench with a good stiff concrete mix. If you are using struts, leave the top two-thirds of the trench unfilled because the bases of the struts will have to be set into this foundation, and it will be filled at this later stage.

The *timber supports* for the structure shown in Fig.2 are of 4in. x 4in. or 100mm x 100mm solid timber. To erect them, cut the three vertical supports to their finished lengths, and then cut the top plate and the two end joists slightly oversize. Paint all the wooden parts with preservative, and soak the foot of each support in a bucket of preservative.

Cut, then fit, the wall plate or joist hangers on the house wall. Whichever you use, they should

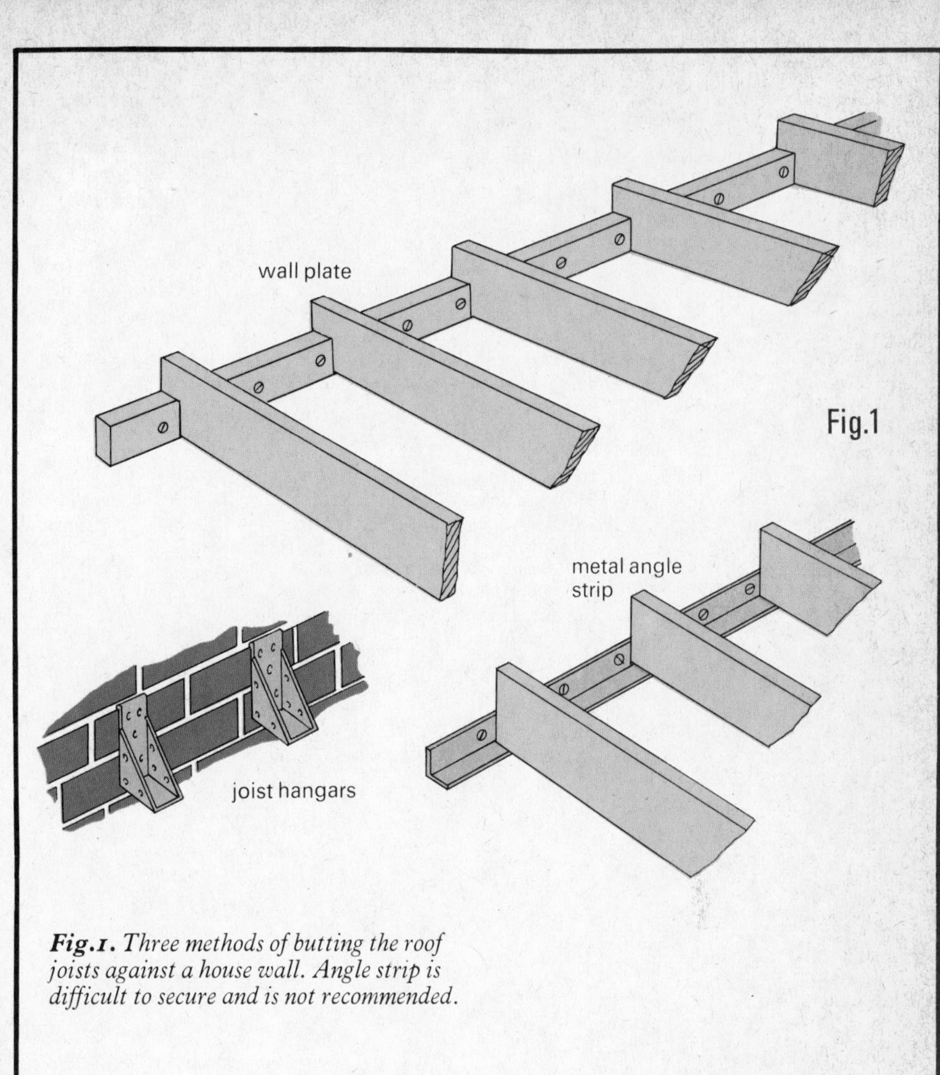

Fig.1. *Three methods of butting the roof joists against a house wall. Angle strip is difficult to secure and is not recommended.*

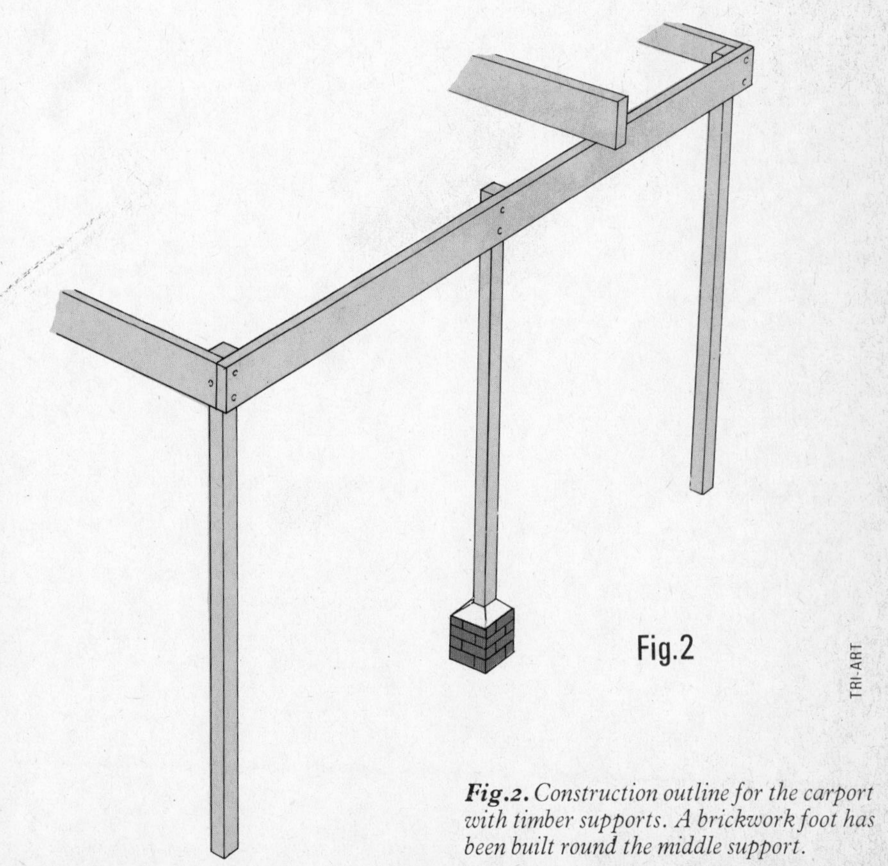

Fig.2. *Construction outline for the carport with timber supports. A brickwork foot has been built round the middle support.*

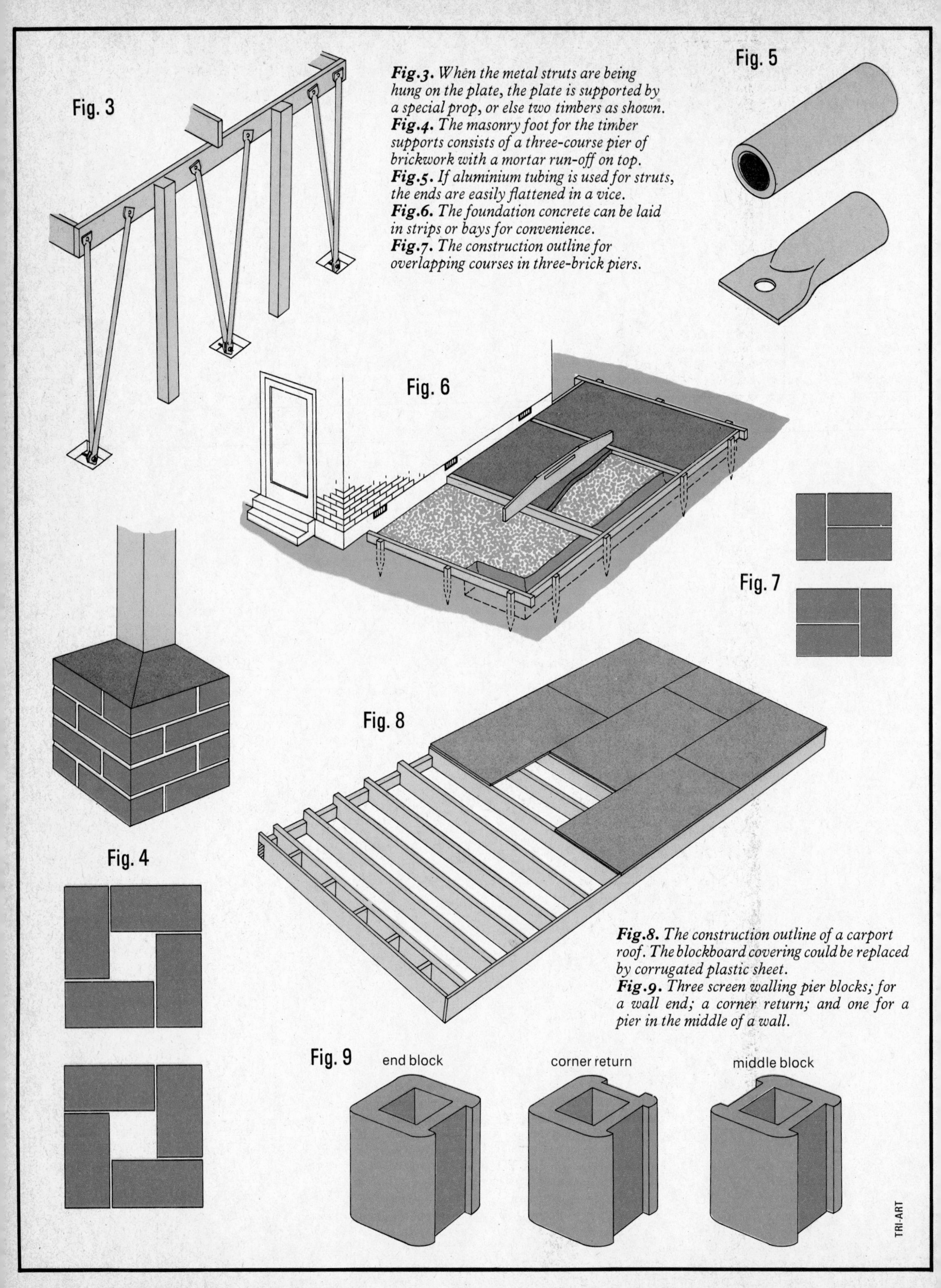

Fig.3. *When the metal struts are being hung on the plate, the plate is supported by a special prop, or else two timbers as shown.*
Fig.4. *The masonry foot for the timber supports consists of a three-course pier of brickwork with a mortar run-off on top.*
Fig.5. *If aluminium tubing is used for struts, the ends are easily flattened in a vice.*
Fig.6. *The foundation concrete can be laid in strips or bays for convenience.*
Fig.7. *The construction outline for overlapping courses in three-brick piers.*

Fig.8. *The construction outline of a carport roof. The blockboard covering could be replaced by corrugated plastic sheet.*
Fig.9. *Three screen walling pier blocks; for a wall end; a corner return; and one for a pier in the middle of a wall.*

be fixed on with No. 10 screws and plastic plugs set in drilled holes.

Lay the three support timbers down on a flat surface—the base of the carport is ideal if it is flat and solid—and nail the joist plate across the tops. You will probably need assistance for the next stage.

Lift the frame upright where it will be housed, nailing bracing struts to hold it temporarily in place if necessary, square it up, then nail the two oversize joists in place, one to each end. Square it again, and it is ready for the brickwork base or foot to be built.

The foot is extremely simple to make; it is only a brickwork box built round the base of the timber, as shown in Fig.4. Build this up for three courses, filling in any inside space between the brickwork and timber with mortar. When this is complete, build a shoulder of mortar at the top, sloping downwards from the timber, so that rain will run off.

When the brickwork mortar has set thoroughly, you can fit the remaining joists in position and complete the rest of the roof.

Strut supports require a slightly different method of construction because they are actually set into the foundation concrete.

The struts can be of $\frac{1}{2}$in. or 35mm mild steel rod, flattened at each end and drilled to take bolts, or of 3in or 75mm aluminium support tube treated in the same way. Steel rod has one great disadvantage—it is hard to cut to length and flatten the ends and this will normally have to be done professionally, whereas aluminium tube can be ordered slightly overlength and cut and shaped on site with equipment no more complicated than a metal vice and a drill, as shown in Fig.5. For this reason the DIY fan will find the tube much more convenient.

It is almost impossible to set the struts in concrete so that they are properly lined up. So the top plate is suspended in its final place, and then the struts are bolted to the plate and dropped into the foundation recess. The lower ends of the struts are then concreted over, embedding them in the correct position.

The main problem is how to support the plate while you are fitting the struts. The best way is to nail the end pair of joists to the wall plate, then lift the other end of the joists and fix them to the house-wall plate with one temporary nail each, so that they pivot. Then you lift the assembly, and hold it in position with proprietary fittings such as Acrow Props. These devices, which are used by builders, are really giant versions of a car jack. In most places they can be hired, and if this is possible take advantage of it; you will need three. Failing this, you can fit two temporary timber supports as shown in Fig.3.

Nail the feet of the props to a length of timber to keep them steady while you draw the temporary nails, push the ends of the rafters into their correct position, and nail them home. When you have tested the roof for level, you can fit the struts. These should have their ends flattened and bolt holes pre-drilled in them.

Hold one of the end vertical struts in position against the plate, and drill a bolt hole through the plate. Push the bolt through, tightening the nut and securing the strut to the plate, and repeat the process with the next strut, which will be located 12in. or 300mm away from the previous strut on the plate, but which will touch it at the bottom, where both enter the same foundation recess.

DOUGLASS BAGLIN

Above. *The design of this carport, and the materials used, have been carefully selected and harmonize perfectly with the house.*

The struts are flattened and drilled for bolts at each end (see Fig.5). At the bottom, each pair should be touching and bolted together, but if your measuring is slightly out don't worry, this is not essential. If the bolt holes do match, secure the struts with a bolt at least 4in. or 100mm long. The idea is to provide a cross-piece so that it will hold in the concrete. If they don't match, fit a 4in. bolt through each hole and place the ends as near as possible.

When you have finished this, the struts will be securely bolted to the top plate and hanging in the foundation recesses underneath, with sturdy bolts fitted through the bottom bolt holes. All that remains to be done is to fill the recesses with concrete—of the same mix as the rest of the the area—and leave this to set. After this, the props or temporary supports can be removed and the rest of the roof fitted.

The heavyweight carport

If you use masonry—bricks, screen walling or whatever—for your roof supports, then you will have to dig more extensive foundations because of the greater weight involved.

One possibility is a strip foundation running under the walls, or under and between piers. But it is much better to do the job thoroughly and lay a strip and raft foundation over the whole area, as shown in Fig.6. A strip foundation presents no great problem, but covering the whole area is quite a task. You can do it in one go, with some very careful planning, or you can do it a bit at a time in bays or panels, as shown in Fig.6. Coat the edge of each panel with a concrete bonding agent before you pour the next one.

Brick piers are a popular form of roof support. If you use this method, build the piers up to the full height of the plates, inserting rag bolts in the top course. The top plate can then be secured to the rag bolts, and the joists and roof fitted.

These piers are of a simple three-brick construction, as shown in Fig.4. They must not be spaced wider apart than 10ft or 3m, but they can be built nearer if you prefer. For example, four piers along a 20ft or 6m carport can look quite attractive with some houses. Decide the number of piers that looks best by means of drawing, as described above.

Screen walling is a very attractive way of providing support for the carport roof. The main disadvantage with this material is that it does not have the strength of brickwork, and the piers—which are specially designed blocks, as shown in Fig.9—must be erected at intervals not exceeding 7ft or 2.1m. And for maximum strength, straight runs of walling are to be avoided. This is the reason for the short return wall of the version in the previous chapter.

Rag bolts for walls are fitted to the top pier block. This is done by placing the block on a flat surface and filling the bottom three-quarters of the hollow in the middle with crumpled newspapers. The remaining third is filled with a concrete or mortar mix in which the rag bolts are suspended during setting, to provide a roof rim or plates.

Variations

There are innumerable variations of the four basic carports shown here. For example, brick piers could be used with the screen walling for extra strength. Or a brick plinth could be built under the screen wall, as shown in the first part of this project. Or if you are using timber supports, you could fit four or five timbers, screw cross braces across or nogging in between them, and board the side over. This arrangement would offer better protection to the car, while avoiding the condensation problem of a garage, which can cause premature rust.

Patio floors and roofs: 1

PROJECT 3

Many gardens are too exposed for sitting out in, except on very hot days. A well constructed and carefully sited patio will give you a secluded and comfortable outdoor living area. Also, a patio will provide you with an ideal spot to keep pot plants and shrubs. With a little imagination in the use of your patio you can bring grace and beauty to your garden.

'Patio' is a Spanish word originally used to describe an open courtyard which many Spanish houses are built around. These provide not only privacy but essential shade from the Spanish sun. The patios you are likely to be more familiar with, however, usually take the form of an open paved terrace adjoining a garden. There are other designs of patio besides the conventional terrace—including open and closed courtyards.

Patios are a practical and attractive idea for any garden. Grass is difficult to keep tidy if it grows right up to the wall of your house and shrubs planted near the house wall might obstruct the view from the windows. A patio will solve these problems for you as well as provide valuable recreation space. Your lawn will be out of action more often than not—either because it is too wet, too soft, for tables and chairs or covered with leaves. Also, your lawn is likely to be too exposed except on very hot still days. A patio is easily maintained and provides a hard, level surface for recreation.

Siting your patio

Before you start to build your patio there are a number of factors you ought to consider. Some of these will conflict so you'll have to decide which of your priorities most demand to be satisfied.

Your individual reasons for deciding to build a patio in the first place will often dictate a suitable site with easy access from the house. If your patio is intended to be purely an extension of your living area it will be best sited so that it has direct access to and from the living room. If this is not possible the patio could be built to adjoin a hall or the dining room or study. If you intend to have meals on your patio in the summer it should also have easy access to the kitchen to simplify the serving of food. A good solution to this problem is to fit a Dutch door in place of your existing kitchen door. This could open directly on to your patio. A dutch door is relatively easy to fit.

If you have children the patio will give them a large, safe playing area, providing the patio is easily visible from the house. You should be able to watch your children play. The kitchen window is usually the best vantage point.

Access to sunshine

The most important point to consider when siting your patio is its access to direct sunlight. In temperate climates a patio should be sited on the south side of the house. However as is most often the case, your patio is likely to be used most in the afternoon and therefore a more westerly position would be better. You are likely to find that neither a southerly or westerly position is compatible with the structure and siting of your house. If access to and from a suitable room is only possible on the east side of the house you could place the patio on that side. If you have to do this be careful to build the patio so that it extends beyond the shadow cast by your house. Some form of effective wind screening may also be necessary with a patio on the east side of the house.

Outlook

Although the structure of your house may make a south facing site possible the view from your patio in this position might well not be very pleasant. The west or east side of your house may on the other hand afford a more pleasant outlook. If this is the case it may be a good idea to sacrifice a certain amount of sunshine for the sake of a better view.

Exposure

The prevailing wind in Britain is usually from a south westerly direction, although this is subject to a few local variations. A patio sited on this side of your house may afford the most sunshine but is likely to be too exposed to the wind except on very calm days. Once again it may be better to choose a different position if it means that your patio will enjoy a sheltered site. This, however, is often not possible for a variety of reasons. If your patio has to be sited on the south west side of your house you can overcome the problem of exposure to excessive wind by installing effective screening. A tall screen sited away from the patio or a lower artificial screen placed closer to it provide equal protection against the wind. Unless you are lucky enough to have some tall trees planted close to the patio already a tree screen will take several years to grow high enough to be of any use. It's a good idea to build a temporary artificial screen which can be taken down as soon as the tree screen is tall enough. Various types of screening are discussed in part 2.

When planting a tree screen choose dense evergreens like cypresses rather than deciduous trees. Evergreens will give good screening all

the year round and they avoid the nuisance of sweeping up piles of fallen leaves.

Privacy

If, after satisfying the other conditions of siting your patio, you find that you still lack privacy, artificial screening from adjoining houses may be necessary. The type, sizes and position of the screening will depend on the degree to which your patio is overlooked as well as the direction. If someone else's garden or

groundfloor windows overlook your patio it will be sufficient to build a vertical screen of approximately 6ft to 7ft (2m) in height extending across the field of view. The clearer the view of your patio your neighbours have, the denser the screening material should be.

If your patio is overlooked from an upstairs window the vertical type of screen will only afford limited protection. Building a higher screen is not often a realistic proposition as it will need to be about 12ft-15ft (4-5m) high.

Above. *This simple but attractive patio has a floor made of ordinary house bricks. Note how the hedges and trees give a rural look to the patio—while providing a very effective windbreak at the same time.*

Use a vertical screen of normal height combined with some kind of open roof screen. These are discussed in part 2.

You should consider the questions of access, sunshine, outlook, exposure and privacy and assess their relative importance before choosing a definite site for your patio.

Size

Once you have chosen a site for your patio you will be able to determine how large it should be. Compared to most building jobs constructing a patio is not expensive so it's best to make it as large as is convenient for your house. Make your patio large enough so that a fair proportion of its area will enjoy sunlight, un-

hindered by shadow, for most of the year. This will depend on how close the house and any free standing walls are to your patio. A well screened patio is very pleasant to sit out on in spring and autumn as well as in high summer. The shadows are much longer in spring and autumn as the sun is lower in the sky. This being the case you should plan your patio at either of these times of the year rather than in summer. If you plan the size and position of your patio in summer you will be very disappointed by the time autumn comes as a much larger area of the patio will be covered in shadow than when you first used it in the summer. You'll find the addition of an extra yard or two to the length and width will make all the difference. The difference in cost is not very much unless you try to add on the extra area when the original patio is complete. Do not aim at having most of the patio area in sunlight. As long as a reasonable area of the floor and one wall are in sunlight the correct impression of brightness will be achieved. If you paint the wall in white or another bright colour sunshine will be reflected to brighten dark areas of the patio.

Try to build your patio to a size that fits in with the size of your garden. If you build a very large patio in a small garden it will not only look ridiculous but will seriously restrict the usefulness of your garden. A town house with a tiny walled garden may look good if the entire garden is paved over. The monotony can be broken by steps, shrubs and perhaps a pool or small fishpond. The intended use of your patio will influence its size. If you only intend to use your patio as an outdoor terrace on which to enjoy meals and light snacks, it need only be large enough for tables and chairs and space to move around. On the other hand if your patio is intended to be a major extension to the living area of your home, incorporating play-space for the children, it will need to be very much larger.

The physical shape of your garden will also influence the size of your patio. For instance, if your garden is on a steep incline the area available for a patio may be strictly limited. Levelling off the garden will involve you in a considerable amount of hard work and in the circumstances it may be better to accept that your patio must, of necessity, be a little on the small side.

Space can be gained by building your patio in a very unconventional shape. Patios don't have to be square. They can equally well be rectangular, oval, hexagonal or even a completely irregular shape. This kind of treatment will be most successful if you follow the natural contours of the ground. An irregularly shaped patio, while providing more actual space, may in fact provide less usable space than a conventional square or rectangular design.

Building the patio floor

Before laying the floor of your patio you must prepare the ground. Usually the patio floor will be on one level except where you wish to incorporate a step. The floor should be on an incline of approximately 1 in 60. This ensures

Left. *A sense of spaciousness is given to this patio by the unusual design of the roof. It provides adequate shade while not totally cutting out the sunlight.*

that rain water will run off.

The ground should be cleared of any old tree roots and rubble. Remove the topsoil and level off the ground to provide a firm base. This should be about 6in. (150mm) lower than the intended level of your finished floor. If the ground is on an incline you'll have to cut deeper at one end than the other to provide a more level base. If the ground is continually wet or of soft earth it may be necessary to dig deeper than 6in. This should then be filled with hardcore to provide a firm base.

When you have levelled off the ground mark out the area of your patio to levels. To do this use wooden pegs of about 2ft (600mm) in length. Drive these into the ground to form a grid. Start with a guide peg at the point of access to your patio. Now drive in another peg about 6ft (2m) away from your guide peg until its top is at the same level. Check this with a spirit level resting on a board placed over the top of the two pegs. Drive in another peg at a right angle to the first. Continue in this way until the pegs form a grid over the whole area of the patio floor.

As mentioned earlier your patio will need to be at a slope of about 1 in 60. A long narrow patio should slope across the shorter dimension and away from the house—causing the rain to run harmlessly to the adjoining garden. This will be all right if the ground is fairly porous. However, if the ground is very dense—like thick clay—it would be better to dig a gulley for the water to run into. This should be placed somewhere near the centre of your patio and the water should run into a drain, a surface water sewer or stream. The gulley should be covered by a removable grid. Gulleying materials are available in stoneware and are similar to a pipe sliced down the middle.

Although patios are normally only subject to foot traffic you may want part of yours to provide parking space for your car. If this is the case, lay an extra surface of concrete over the hardcore and under the paving. A slab of about 4in. (100mm) thick should be sufficient in most cases. If the ground is exceptionally soft or spongy it may be a good idea to reinforce the concrete with steel mesh. The concrete should be laid on a well packed bed of hardcore at least 6in. (150mm) thick. You can lay the paving loose over the concrete—in a bed of sand for instance. The paving can then be lifted as necessary when further conversion is necessary. If your patio has to bear the weight of a car at any time, the paving should be laid in a sand and cement mix mortar.

A good DIY manual will describe paving techniques in greater detail.

When deciding on the exact size of your patio, try to make it a multiple of the size of your paving stones. For instance, if you intend to use 2ft x 2ft (600mm x 600mm) slabs you could make your patio 36ft x 10ft (11m x 3m). This would require 5 rows of 18 slabs—totalling 90 slabs in all. You will have to make allowances if you intend to install a pool or have plants growing direct from the ground incorporated into your patio. It also might be a good idea to have more slabs than you need as they are very solid and attractive and are therefore excellent for building a low stone wall along one or two sides, or planters such as in chapter 1 may be used.

PAF INTERNATIONAL

Above. *Creepers and pot plants are used to good effect with this traditional style of patio. The original Spanish conception of an enclosed courtyard—offering both shade and privacy—is preserved in this patio.*

Below. *Here the kitchen door opens onto this well-constructed patio. Creeping plants adorn the low stone wall, the pillars and the open timber roof—providing shade as well as beauty in almost any garden.*

SYNDICATION INTERNATIONAL

Patio floors and roofs: 2

Part one of this chapter dealt with the siting, preparation of the ground, and the layout of the patio. This, the second part, describes the best materials to use for paving, what shrubs to grow, how to lay out a pool or fishpond, and aspects of patio roof design.

As mentioned in part one it is essential to decide on the size, shape and siting of your patio before starting to build it. Try to decide what you want at the outset as alterations to the finished patio can involve you in a lot of expense and hard work.

Paving

It's best to use one material in a roughly uniform colour to pave the patio. Different coloured paving stones, unless carefully used, will destroy any harmony that the shape of the patio should have with the site. The use of different coloured stones can work with a very large patio floor. A big expanse of grey paving stones can look rather dull so it's a good idea to relieve the monotony with small, regularly shaped, areas of coloured stone. You could use house bricks or cobbles set into the floor to achieve the same effect. A good alternative is to omit some of the paving stones and plant flowers or small shrubs in the spaces left. Don't plant shrubs which will grow to a large size as the roots may lift the paving stones. Also, very large plants will look out of place and will cover your patio with dead leaves. Evergreens such as heather are a good choice for patios as they will not shed their leaves or develop large roots. Some evergreens will flower in shaded areas of the patio. Apart from these permanent plants you can add different annuals each year. Plants like phlox, nemesia and lobelia are good for patios as they won't grow too large in one season and they contrast well with paving. They also brighten up shaded areas considerably. The gaps you leave in the paving for plants should be filled with a good compost to a depth of approximately 9in. (215mm). Before you place the soil make sure that you remove all the cement and sand used in laying the patio floor. Use plants like clematis and honeysuckle to cover walls and windbreaks near the patio. These plants are climbers and will spread quickly, providing very attractive foliage and flowers.

Left. *The exotic appearance of this patio is enhanced by the open timber roof. Stone support columns, and well placed creeping plants, lend a rustic look to this corner of the garden, providing both shelter and privacy.*

ELSA M. MEGSON

Paving materials

Pre-cast concrete slabs are available in ordinary grey and in a number of tinted shades including red, green and blue. You should be careful in the use of coloured slabs as they can look garish when mixed together.

Slabs are available in a number of sizes—12in. x 12in. (300mm x 300mm), 12in. x 18in. (300mm x 450mm), 24in. x 24in. (600mm x 600mm) and 36in. x 24in. (900mm x 600mm). Two thicknesses are available—1¼in. (38mm) and 2in. (50mm). Apart from square and rectangular slabs you can also get round and hexagonal shapes.

Original and interesting designs for paving can be achieved by combining differently shaped slabs, or, instead of simply laying the slabs in the conventional way you could stagger the joins. Staggering the joins means that instead of the slabs meeting corner to corner the joins are staggered in alternate rows.

Coloured slabs can be effectively used by making an inset pattern with them. The best way of doing this is to sketch the pattern onto a piece of paper. This way you can decide how many stones will need to be cut. Cutting the stones is a tricky business as they can split easily. It's best to get a local mason to do it for you. If you want to cut the stones yourself cut a groove line in the slab with a bolster and tap along the groove line with a heavy mallet.

Because *natural stone* has to be quarried and cut to shape, it tends to be quite expensive. This is especially true if the stone comes from a long way from where you live as the weight makes haulage a costly business. If a suitable stone is available in your own area you can often get it cheaply. If you arrange your own transport you can get stone cheaply by collecting it direct from the quarry.

Many local stones are available and look most attractive when toned in with your house stone. They are much more appealing than plain concrete. Slate is often very suitable if it is available. Your priority must be how easily it can be transported, and whether it comes in the correct size and thickness. Consult your local builder's merchant for choices.

Some stone comes in roughly squared slabs and others in irregular shapes. Natural stone looks best when not combined with another material. Subtle colour changes, inherent in the stone, will provide all the variety necessary.

Apart from large slabs of natural stone some *small stones* are available. You can use these smaller stones to lay a border as a contrast to the main floor.

Granite setts were once used for paving highways and are ideal for use on patios. These

BILL MACLAUGHLIN

consist of hewn cubes of stone about 4in. (11mm) square and can be laid in straight joints or bonded. You can also lay them in a fan or a circular pattern. They give an uneven surface which is uncomfortable to walk on but useful as a border or an inset. Flint cobbles or ballast rejects are easily obtainable and are of a similar appearance to granite setts when laid.

Brick is a suitable paving material and is available in a wide range of colours. However, because of the small size of bricks, paving a whole patio with them is rather hard work, and in the case of a large patio a floor made entirely of brick will tend to look out of place. Ordinary house bricks can be used for paving provided they are hard and well burnt. If the bricks are too soft frost will make them flake and crack. Besides house bricks you can get *brick 'pavers'* —made specially for this use. 'Pavers' are approximately 2in. (50mm) thick and are available in biscuit, browns or blue-grey colours.

If you intend to use ordinary house bricks they should be laid either with the moulded recess ('frogs') facing downwards, or, on edge. Before you decide on how you are going to lay the bricks you should first work out the number you'll need. A typical patio floor covering an area of, say, 20ft x 12ft (6100mm x 3650mm) will require approximately 860 bricks if laid flat and about 1300 laid on edge.

Laying

The foundation of your patio floor must be firm, level and well drained. Unless part of your patio will have to take the weight of a car, a bed of well packed hardcore will be sufficient as a foundation for the floor. Setting out the floor should be tackled very carefully, and construction details must be checked.

When laying the foundation, ram the hardcore down with a tamping beam. With certain types of hardcore an ordinary garden roller will be all right for this job. The firmness of the soil also has a bearing on this. If your soil is quite soft a garden roller will certainly be suitable for packing the hardcore.

When the hardcore has been laid level and well packed you can begin paving. As your patio will probably only have to bear the weight of foot traffic you need only lay a bed of a suitable mortar mix. The paving stones are laid over this bed. Cementing the stones in place is not usually necessary if the bed is firm and level. Also, uncemented stones will enable you to alter the shape of the floor more easily should you want to later on.

The patio roof

The most common type of patio roof is one made of timber joists with gaps left open to the sky—something like a pergola. It's probably best to have a covered section at one end to provide shade on very hot days. A covered section will also give you more privacy as it will restrict the view from neighbouring upstairs windows.

The covered section could be made from a solid material, but a sheet of canvas is easier to fix and has the added advantage of being movable.

The timber joists can be fixed either running parallel along the length of the patio, or across its width with a distance of about a foot between each joist.

The best size for the joists is about 4in. x 1in. (100mm x 25mm) and they should be fixed so that the narrow edges face the sky and the patio floor.

Once the roof has been built you can use creeping plants both to give colour and beauty to the roof and provide extra shade.

An alternative to the fixed timber patio roof is to fix a canvas awning. This could be striped, patterned or in a plain colour. An awning has a number of advantages over the fixed type of roof—it is movable, easily fixed and cheaper than a timber roof.

Pools

If your patio is to be fairly large you might consider installing a pool. Choose a site for the pool carefully and dig the hole to the required shape, depth and size. A depth of about 9in. (225mm) should be sufficient for the pool. Dig the hole to an extra 6in. depth as the surface of the water should be below the level of the patio floor.

The sides of the pool should slope in slightly so the hole should be wider at the top than at the bottom. If the sides of the pool are sloped in this way, ice will be less likely to form as it will slip up the sides of the pool as it expands and will therefore break up.

Once you have made the hole an even shape sprinkle sand or sifted earth around its sides. The hole should now be lined with a heavy duty plastic sheeting temporarily held in place at the top with bricks. Press the sheeting to the sides of the hole so that it moulds to the shape of the pool. The area around the top of the pool should now be paved. This will hold the sheeting in place at the top. Now fill the pool slowly with water. Pool construction is described more fully in later chapters.

The most popular plants for pools are water lilies. These look very striking and are available with yellow, white or red flowers. Besides water lilies there are a huge variety of water plants for you to choose from.

A number of cold blooded fish are suitable for outdoor pools. These include goldfish, shubunkins, golden rudd, green tench and golden orfe. If you wish to have fish it is important that you prevent the pool from freezing over in winter as this would reduce the amount of oxygen getting to the water. A small electric heater floating on the surface will do the trick.

If you wish to make your pool less static and a little more interesting fit a submerged electric pump fed from the mains by an insulated cable. If you do this you will be able to incorporate such things as a fountain or small waterfalls into the construction of your pool.

Left. *The white brick of the windbreak wall is also used as a material for the built-in barbecue. The brilliant white contrasts well with the grey slabs of the patio floor.*
Inset left. *This pool is brought to life by colourful plants in and around the water. The waterfall gives a realistic impression of a tranquil country spring.* ***Right.*** *Plants and shrubs add interest to this patio. These can be placed either in tubs and pots or planted in beds in the patio floor.*

ZEFA

Above. *This attractive sun room is inexpensively built. The existing structure of the house means that only two external walls to the room have to be constructed.*

People appreciate sunshine. With more leisure time now available, there is a greater incentive for home owners to design ways of bringing the sun into their homes as well as enjoying it on vacation. A well planned sun room can make a useful leisure space linking house and garden as well as providing you with a place to soak up the sun.

The room should be designed to collect as much sunlight as possible, and it must therefore be situated on the side of the house which faces the sun for most of the day. In the northern hemisphere this will be the south side, and in the southern hemisphere the north.

Basing the position of the main windows as near to south or north as possible will provide the maximum total number of hours of sunlight inside the room, but you may prefer to vary this a little to suit your own needs. If the room is likely to be empty during the morning and only used in the afternoon and early evening, it might be better to face the main windows to the south-west, or even due west in countries where the days are very long in summer (this includes Britain). But if you intend to use the room intermittently all day, a main south window will probably offer the best solution. Depending on the position of the sun room in the house, it may be possible to have a smaller window in the west wall as well, or even in both east and west walls.

Although the orientation of the room (which determines the quantity of sunlight) is often the major factor in siting a sun room, the view is also important, and may to a certain extent override orientation in deciding the location of the room and its windows. If the southern outlook is poor, but that to the east or west more attractive, it may be worth sacrificing some sunlight in order to enjoy a pleasant view. Though a north window alone would not catch any sun in the northern countries, an additional window in a north wall looking out to a sunlit garden beyond the immediate shadow of the house, may be worth considering as a second window position in conjunction with a main west or (where possible) south window.

SYNDICATION INTERNATIONAL

Above. *This ordinary semi-detached house has been transformed by the addition of a sun room. Designs such as this are suitable for most houses—large or small.*

Choosing the position

When you are choosing the position for a sun room, you will have to consider a number of factors, and will have to assess which are the most important in your own case to reach a suitable compromise. Firstly, as discussed above, there is the need to choose a position which will permit the maximum amount of sunlight to enter the room, and secondly, the relationship of the room with the garden. These two factors may have to be considered together with other factors to give a reasonable amount of sunlight and a good outlook.

Remember that tall trees, especially if fairly near the house, could obstruct sunlight. The sun's angle is much lower in winter than in summer, and a tree which may be well below the sun in midsummer and throw only a short shadow could cut out the sun during the winter months when the shadow will stretch much further. This is especially true of evergreen trees.

The third factor to be borne in mind is also an external one: the question of exposure. In Britain, north-facing sites are likely to be much more exposed to cold winds than south-facing ones, although other factors such as nearby walls and buildings can affect this. The cold winds will reduce the inside temperature of the room mostly during the winter months, when it will only be used internally, but may also be a disadvantage in summer when the room will normally be used in conjunction with outside seating on a terrace.

So a clump of tall evergreen trees which could represent a shadow nuisance on the south side of a garden may be a decided advantage as a windbreak along the north or east side, where their shadows will fall away from the house in the afternoon anyway. If there are no such trees it may be worth planting some, and using a temporary additional screen until they grow tall enough to be effective. This can also be made up of natural planting, for instance quick-growing plants that can be removed later.

Alternatively, it can consist of a perforated wall made from precast concrete screen wall units, or an open timber screen with climbing plants. If more substantial protection is needed, a panel of vertical timber louvres placed at 45° and angled so that it presents an unbroken face to the wind can be both attractive and effective. This type of screen forms a good end-stop to a paved terrace.

If really severe wind conditions prevail, it may be advisable to use a solid brick or stone wall. To relieve the heaviness of its appearance, you can leave small openings and stand flower boxes in them, or make small beds for trailing plants in the top of the wall.

If two alternative positions seem equally suitable as far as these points are concerned, other factors can be decisive. Something which could tip the balance in favour of one site or the other is the existing wall pattern. If one position involves building against a flat wall and the other in an internal angle between two existing walls, the second has the advantage of requiring the building of only two new walls instead of three. Apart from the resultant saving in construction cost, a room in an internal angle is more comfortable and less expensive to heat, as it has only two external walls instead of three. It also offers two directions of access from the main house instead of one.

This factor of access is another major consideration. When a new room is being built into an external wall, it is often hard to give it an independent entrance from the hall that does not involve going through another room. So it may be necessary to approach the sun room through an existing room. Many people find access through a living or dining room acceptable, but if you do not, and practical considerations prevent entry through other rooms such as study or kitchen, the only solution is to cut a new corridor by partitioning off a 3ft (900mm) wide strip of an existing room between the hall and sun room.

You will also have to think about the effect the sun room will have on the room or rooms adjacent to it. In a house with large rooms, there may be a piece of solid external wall long enough to accommodate the whole of the new room without cutting into existing windows. In most cases, however, and particularly since the sun room will normally have its longer side parallel with the external wall, at least part of an existing window or external door is affected.

If this is the only source of light to the existing room, the addition of the new room will seriously reduce the level of daylight even if the window is only partly blocked. You can compensate for this by creating a new window in a wall not affected by the new room. Sometimes, if the existing rooms have high ceilings, a clerestory window can be cut in the external wall of the inside room over the roof of the sun room, allowing direct high-level lighting.

If neither of these solutions is practicable, you can ensure that ample light enters indirectly from the sun room by using large windows in the wall adjoining the inside room. You will have to open up most of the area of the wall between the old and new rooms in order to admit as much light as possible. The use of rooflights in the sun room roof, as mentioned later, can also help to boost light to an inside room lit in this way.

In summer, the sun room will probably be used for many activities, and you will tend to use it in conjunction with the garden, so there will be fairly heavy traffic in and out. In the cold months, on the other hand, you are more likely to use it for sitting in to enjoy a touch of sunlight. So you should choose finishes, especially for the floor, which are tough enough to withstand traffic from the garden yet comfortable enough to make an attractive retreat in spring and autumn. Carpet may therefore be less suitable than, for example, foam-backed vinyl flooring or sealed cork.

The wall finish, too, should be durable, and here you could use a vinyl-faced paper or cloth. When considering fabrics, remember that though most modern carpets and materials are colour-fast, some dyes can still be bleached by strong sunlight.

Fitting the windows

To let in plenty of sun, you will have to be generous with windows. These would normally extend from near the ceiling, with only a lintel above to support the roof, to a sill which can be as low as 1ft (300mm) or 1ft 6in. (450mm) above floor level. You could fit bookshelves or shallow cupboards under the windows to provide a wide internal sill, which will be useful for potted plants. Alternatively, the space under the windows can be used for heating units, as discussed below.

The windows themselves should have a fair proportion of opening sashes. British building regulations require habitable rooms to have openable windows totalling at least one-twentieth of the floor area, but sun rooms usually need a much higher proportion to avoid unpleasant heat build-up on hot days. You could aim at having half the windows openable. They can be of many types, including side-hung, centre-pivoted, top-hung (hinged along the top edge) or horizontally-sliding.

In countries where large windows would admit very strong sunlight for prolonged periods, it may be necessary to damp it down at times. This can be done with permanent filtering through the use of special glass, or variable control by means of venetian or roller blinds, or folding canvas blinds or shutters mounted externally. In equatorial countries, *brise-soleils* are often used; these are projecting canopies or vertical ribs permanently incorporated into the structure which restrict the entry of sunlight into the rooms in varying degrees, depending on the position of the sun.

You will want at least one external door

Above. *The clean lines of this sun room blend well with the rest of the house. Picture windows at each end of the room give uninterrupted views of the well-wooded garden.*

ARCHITECTURE AND LANDSCAPE LIBRARY

giving access to the garden or terrace, and this will also provide ventilation when open. But remember that there are many occasions when you will want ventilation without opening the door, so don't rely on it too much. The door will normally be a single side-hung door or pair of doors in wood or metal, either partly or fully-glazed. But an alternative which is becoming increasingly popular is a panel of full-height fully-glazed horizontally-sliding doors. These consist of two, three or more panels which slide across each other, or a pair of panels which slide across fixed lights at each side. They give a fully-glazed effect from floor to ceiling, and if required from wall to wall.

Two characteristics of this type of panel should be borne in mind: first, the type in which all the panels slide will not allow the whole width to open: there will always be slightly more than the width of one panel obstructed; and on a type with only two sliding panels, this will permit slightly less than half the total width to open. A 12ft wide panel of the two-panel type will therefore only allow about 5ft 6in. clear opening in the centre.

Second, the rate of heat loss through single glass is some four to five times that of a conventional cavity wall, so that large areas of single glazing will be cold to sit near and will cool the room as a whole. Equally, they may make the room too warm on hot, sunny days. If you intend to use the sun room only on warm days there is no great disadvantage in using large areas of single glazing, but if you want to be able to sit in it during spring and autumn in temperate climates, it would be a disadvantage.

The usual solution to this problem is to use double-glazed panels. These consist of two sheets of glass about $\frac{1}{4}$in. (6mm) thick, with an airspace between containing dry air. The air is an effective heat insulator, both reducing the heat loss from the room and preventing condensation on the inside face, because it is comparatively warm, and on the outside, because the contained air is dry. These are, however, almost twice as expensive and twice as heavy as single-glazed units.

Double-glazed panels cut the heat loss to about half that of single glazing, but this is still about twice that of most solid walls. So unless the situation is very sheltered and faces due south you would be best advised to restrict the area of full-height glazing to the warmest side of the room, and use conventional windows (also double-glazed) elsewhere.

Walls facing the coldest side should be without glazing as a rule, and of cavity construction. For the outer leaf, you can use facing bricks if they will blend well with the existing house, or else common bricks or concrete blocks finished with rendering, boarding, tile- or slate-hanging. The inner leaf should be of lightweight concrete block, which will help to reduce the heat loss. The cavity between the two leaves can be filled with a thermal insulator such as injected urea formaldehyde foam which will reduce the heat loss still further. But take care not to use an insulator that will create a moisture bridge between the two leaves.

Roofing the sun room

The treatment of the roof will depend on the original house. If the sun room is a single-storey ground-floor extension to a 2 or 3 storey house a flat roof will probably provide the best solution. This is cheaper to construct than a pitched roof, and will often blend in better. If you want to match an existing tiled or slated main roof, the pitch would have to be similar for reasons of appearance, but this, too, is likely to look rather awkward in a small extension, especially if the main roof has the usual plain tiles with a pitch of about 40°. A pitched roof could also interfere with existing windows on the first floor of the house.

The flat roof has a number of advantages. It can be strengthened and used as a roof terrace to a bedroom above if you add an external door, or rooflights can be incorporated. This can be attractive in the sun room itself, especially if it is rather deep, and is particularly useful where the existing room behind loses much of the daylight it previously enjoyed. A row of square rooflights or a continuous length of 'patent glazing' near the wall of the inside room, used in conjunction with a large opening or glazed panel in the interior wall, will let plenty of light in to the inside room.

The traditional finish for flat roofs is three-layer built-up bituminous felt. If you lay it correctly in dry weather, it should give years of trouble-free service. Recently, however, a more durable material has been introduced which is laid in a single layer, and this appears to be an improvement. If the roof is to be used as a terrace, you should lay asbestos-cement or other lightweight paving slabs over the sheet roofing. In all cases the roof must have a slope of at least

1 in 60 to a gutter drained by a rainwater pipe which discharges to a surface-water drain or a soakaway.

Heating

A sun room is likely to have rather intermittent use, possibly being occupied for several days in succession during a warm spell, and then being empty for a while. A permanent heating system is thus not really appropriate, although if there is an existing hot-water central-heating system you may be able to extend it to one or two radiators in the new room, which can be turned off when not required. This may be difficult, though, either because long flow-and-return runs would be necessary from the nearest circuit, or because the boiler has no spare capacity. The same problem may arise in extending a ducted warm-air system. And other types of heating, such as storage heaters or embedded floor-warming, are also unsuitable because they cannot be turned on quickly.

Some form of local self-contained heater will usually offer the best solution. The most convenient are electric appliances: conventional convector heaters can be fitted at low level along walls or under windows; or you can use fan-assisted convectors which have the advantage of heating the room up quickly from cold. If you want to, you can control these with a time-clock or thermostat. They are also useful for circulating cool air in hot weather. Other possibilities are a combined radiant and convector or a simple radiant electric heater.

If you cannot build a separate sun room on to your house, you may be able to make one from another space. Some older houses have a conservatory or verandah which with minor improvements could become a most attractive sun room. It will probably need a new roof, windows and doors, and some redecorating work, but the cost should be well repaid in converting a previously wasted space into a room which has real usefulness, and which adds to the value of the house without the expense of building a new addition.

Another possibility for making a sun room at reduced cost is where a new extension is already being added to an old house. The two different parts can easily be linked by a glazed passage incorporating an entrance area, and if this is widened beyond the size of a basic hall or corridor it can form a pleasant sun room, providing it catches enough sun. Either the whole entrance area can be enlarged, or the sun room can be arranged to open off the back of it: this second plan has the advantage of the sun room being independent of the other rooms, and it gives a pleasant impression when entering the house through the new hall. The remarks above concerning windows, doors, finishes, wall and roof construction and heating are all equally applicable in this case.

You will probably want to use your sun room in conjunction with the garden in summer, and a paved terrace surrounding it can be very useful, both as a dry and level area for sitting and for children to play on, and for reducing the dirt carried into the house from the garden itself. The terrace should be wide enough to enjoy plenty of sun, allowance being made for the shadow of the other parts of the house, and screened from cold winds. It should be on one continuous level as far as possible, with only a fall of about 1 in 60 to throw off rainwater. Small terraces can be drained by sloping them away from the house towards the garden, but large terraces should fall to a central gulley with a drain leading to a soakaway or main drain.

Natural stone slabs look very attractive remember there are many different types and colours of stone apart from your local stone or concrete. But for large areas stone will be very expensive, and the commonest material used today is precast concrete slabs. These are usually 1ft or 2ft square (300mm or 600mm), or 3ft x 2ft (900mm x 600mm), but they can also be obtained in hexagonal, circular and other shapes, and in a choice of colours.

The terrace can be made more attractive by leaving out a slab here and there and planting small alpine or rock plants, or by making decorative panels of brickwork, cobbles or setts (square road blocks). If the garden is on a slope, you may have to cut into a bank at some point in order to maintain a level terrace, and this will also involve containing the higher earth with a retaining wall.

Above. *The conservatory of this large old house, whose sheltered position is provided by the main building, has been renovated into a spacious sun room.*

This should be built on a concrete foundation below the terrace level in 9in. (225mm) thick brickwork or stonework.

Piers may be needed at intervals, especially if the wall is more than a few courses high. The weight of wet soil can be considerable, and it is important to make sure that a retaining wall is stiff enough to resist its tendency to overturn under this weight. Consult a builder if you are in any doubt.

If the garden falls away from the house, the terrace will have to be built up on a similar wall, and if there is a considerable drop, it may be advisable to build a safety barrier, especially if young children will use the area. This could take the form of a handrail with closely-spaced uprights or substantial horizontal rails, or perforated screen walling, or otherwise a low solid wall, which can be of cavity construction to allow planting along its centre.

PROJECT 5

Free standing swimming pools

A swimming pool gives a new dimension to your life. It greatly increases your recreational facilities and adds value to your home. And with the development of free standing pools, you can give a touch of luxury to your home for a fraction of the cost of conventional pools.

Free standing swimming pools have many advantages over conventional, sunken, pools. They are portable, attractively finished and strong but fairly light. They are very much cheaper than ordinary pools—sometimes as little as a quarter of the cost. In addition, free standing pools usually stand above ground which is a lot safer if there are toddlers around.

The installation of free standing swimming pools is straightforward, requiring no major excavation or plumbing. They take up less space than conventional pools and are ideal for smaller gardens.

Planning the pool

To make a real success of your pool you must plan the project thoroughly. The positioning of the pool is very important here, as a badly placed pool will soon fall into disuse, especially if it is simply tacked on at the bottom of the garden.

The best place for a pool is an open sunny spot that is sheltered from the breeze and yet is

Below. *A pool in the medium price range. It can be put up in a few days, with a capacity of around 11,000 gallons. A boardwalk is a very suitable addition for children, as then steps are not the sole point of easy entry.*

CRANLEIGH POOLS LTD., CALCOT, READING

relatively accessible. Trees make ideal wind breaks but don't put the pool near an overhanging tree as the leaf fall will cause unnecessary cleaning work. Alternatives to trees as wind breaks are lattice style screen walling or birch lap fencing.

To find the best site, make a scaled plan of your garden. Take the measurements and mark the positions of the main features—the house, trees, paths, fences, walls and steps. Also mark on it the estimated position of septic tanks or underground sewerage or drainage pipes. You must, of course, avoid putting the pool over these. Then make a cardboard or paper cutout of the pool and try it in different positions on the garden plan. When you have decided on a site, study it for a few days to see where the house and tree shade falls. One point to remember though—small children need supervision and putting the pool within sight of the house is a valuable safety factor.

Your swimming pool will need a hard surround at least 2ft (610mm) and a sunbathing area—a level, well trimmed lawn or patio nearby. You can landscape the pool with a combination of screen walling, low growing coniferous shrubs or thicket plants, or a rockery, to help give the pool a luxurious setting.

Don't put sweet smelling plants close to the pool as these attract bees and wasps. Prickly or thorny bushes or trees with surface roots too near the pool will soon cause inconvenience.

Types of pool available

There are many different types of free standing pools on the market. Trade associations of pool manufacturers can provide details of these. There are, however, three main types of pool.

The temporary, or Splasher, pool is erected and filled when you want to use it. Usually, they do not have a filtration system and have to be emptied to clean. They do, however, require chlorination (see below) since, even though they may not be up for long at any one time, bacteria collect and can make the water unsafe.

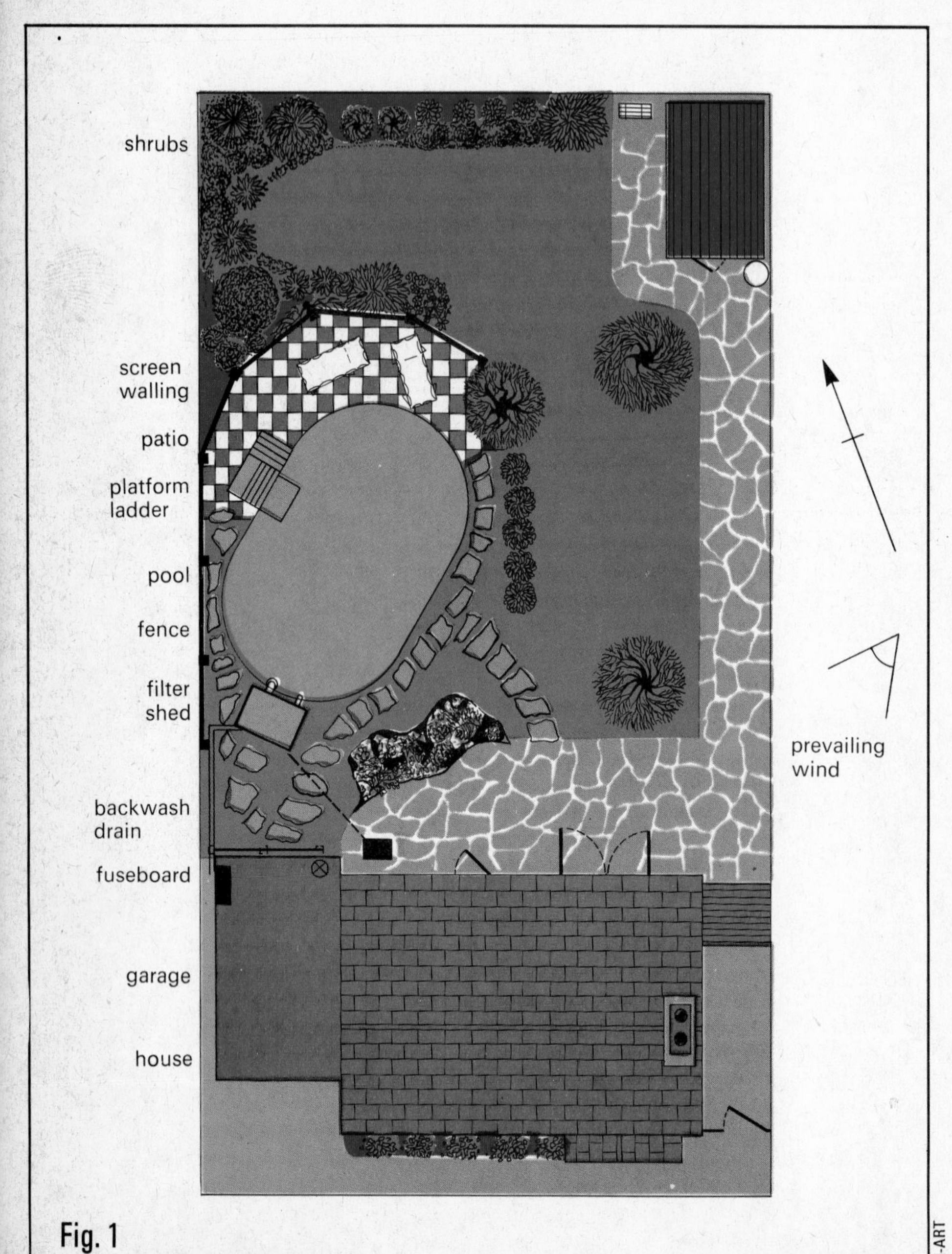

Fig.1. A garden layout showing many of the best design features. The pool is sheltered from the wind by a fence, trees are sited so that leaf fall will be carried away from the pool, there is a paved patio for sunbathing and the pool is close enough to the house to allow you to keep an eye on the children. When you are planning a pool draw a garden map like this —it will solve many of the design problems.
Fig.2. The ground under the pool must be perfectly level—if it slopes the weight of the water will put a great strain on one of the pool walls. Prepare the site using a spirit level to check that the ground is level.

The lightweight portable pool has a flexible steel side wall and a supporting structure that can be erected once the ground has been prepared. These pools take a day or two to fill and then a few more days for the water to warm up.

Sometimes mains water is cloudy and it helps to pre-clean it by filling the pool through a porous bag containing some diatomaceous earth. This is a fine powder composed of tiny sea plants and consisting of silica or opal that filters bacteria from water.

The larger pools of this type have a capacity of between 10,000 and 12,000 gallons or 45,500-54,500 litres. You need some sort of filtration system with this type of pool and the water should be chlorinated.

The heavy duty portable pool has interlocking prefabricated plywood wall panels, or concrete sections with a maximum weight of 2cwt (102kg). These are supported by steel stan-

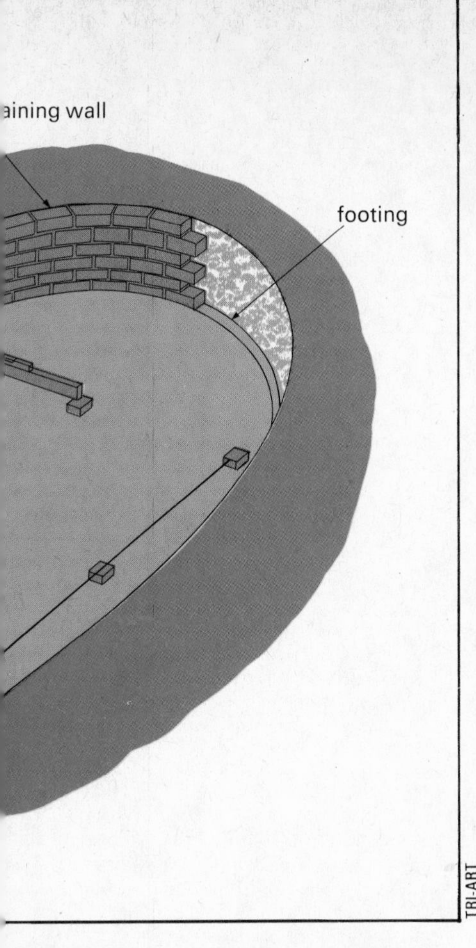

Right. *An oval pool, formed by joining two halves of a circular pool at either end of a rectangular pool. Notice here the concrete edging running all the way round, the fence and trees at the back serving as a windbreak, and the very practical horizontal railing.*

chions to form a box beam structure, with buttresses to prevent the sides spreading.

These pools are designed for school as well as for family use, so the filter system and equipment is stronger than for other types of free standing pools. The pools are modular in design so they can be extended up to a maximum residential size of 45ft (13.7m) with a capacity of 20,000 gallons (90900 l).

Equipment

Essential equipment, such as the filtration system and pool liner, must be hard wearing and resistant to the corrosive action of water. The filtration system should be able to cope with the full amount of water and the pool liner should resist ultra-violet rays—most suppliers now give a ten year guarantee on this point. There should not be any sharp edges or bolts in the pool.

Probably the most useful accessory for a free standing pool is a heater. This adds about six weeks to the swimming season in the spring and autumn but you will need a pool cover to reduce heat loss from the pool surface. Pool decking and ladders are useful, particularly for the less agile. A skimmer, to collect surface debris and leaves from the filtration system, and an underwater vacuum cleaner will help keep the pool clean and tidy.

Preparation

You do not have to get planning permission for free standing pools but, as with any structure you build, you should check what the by-laws stipulate in your area. In the case of swimming pools you should inform the water authority of your plans—they may wish to install a meter.

When the pool kit is delivered, check all the items and read the manufacturer's directions carefully. These give full instructions on the erection and maintenance of the pool.

There are, however, several points that you should be particularly careful about:

—make sure that there are water and electrical services near the planned position of the pool. The filter will have to be backwashed, that is, the flow of the filter reversed to clear waste material from the mechanism, and if you cannot use the drains to get rid of this matter, then a small backwash soakaway can be built. An ideal size for this is 2ft x 2ft x 2ft (610mm x 610mm x 610mm).

—pool liners should not be set directly into gravel, asphalt or tar, or on ground recently treated with weedkiller.

—if the pool is to be set into a slope, surface drainage water should be channelled around, and not into, the pool.

—clear all weeds and stones from the area in which the pool is to be set. A concrete base for the pool is not essential, a loamy soil being ideal provided it is tamped down.

—the bottom of the pool area must be level. This is a very important job since a tilting swimming pool will throw considerable weight onto one side. This could cause it to fail.

—if you want your pool to be set into a slope you must dig out the slope. Do not create a slope by making up ground. Water weighs $\frac{3}{4}$ tons (762kg) per cu yd and it will cause the pool to sink.

—if any of the banks around the pool are more than 1ft (305mm) high, build retaining walls to stop soil washing down into the pool.

—the base rails of some makes of pool have to

CHRISTAL POOLS, WEST HAGLEY, WORCS.

be set on concrete blocks. Sets of blocks should be parallel and you can check this by measuring the diagonals. If the soil is wet or loamy, set the blocks in a concrete mix.

If your pool is of the type that is set partially in the ground the following points are important:

—reinforced concrete should be used in retaining walls.

—you must provide adequate drainage to carry away surface water.

—high water tables present considerable problems but ways of overcoming this are discussed in later chapters.

—the Splasher pool and the lightweight portable must not be set into the ground.

Erecting the pool

Again, you should follow the manufacturer's instructions closely when putting your swimming pool kit together and in place.

Erect the pool around the required amount of soft sand for the floor—the required depth is

18 sq yds or 16 sq m.

Set the perimeter rails absolutely level, fit the stanchions and corner posts and install the side panels or uncoil the sheeting. Secure the sides to the framework. Cover the area with fine, damp sifted soil for the floor covering and then spread and tamp down the soil underlay.

A sunny day is ideal for lining the pool as vinyl sheeting will soften in the warmth and become more pliable. Wear soft soled shoes also, to guard against tearing the pool lining.

With adhesive tape, stick the liner edges to the pool wall, lining up the inlet/outlet holes in the liner with those in the pool walls. Cover the floor with 1in. (25mm) of water and smooth out any wall creases. Continue to fill the pool, smoothing out creases after every 12in. (305mm) of water. Roll the liner edges over the top of the pool and double the edges over before fixing the top rail coping. If your particular make of pool requires it, use non-corrosive nails or staples to fix the lining at the top.

If your ground work was accurate and level, the full pool should show a level water line. The pool liner is now protected by the water which cushions it against sharp objects. If a tear develops later, though, it can be easily repaired with a piece of vinyl and the manufacturer's recommended adhesive.

***Right.** A standard circular pool, which has been imaginatively landscaped into the side of a grassed slope. Allowance has been made for a foot bath, to wash off any loose dirt before it is carried into the water.*

Filtration systems

A filter system is essential if your pool's capacity is more than 2,000 gallons (9090 l). Splasher pools, which don't have a filter, need to be emptied about once a month and filtered pools should be cleaned thoroughly once a year. A filter is a mechanical cleaner which removes dust, dirt and dead algae—the water in unfiltered pools soon becomes cloudy and unwholesome. Even if you have a filter you must still treat the water chemically to kill bacteria and insects (see below).

Some manufacturers specify that their filter systems should run continuously—they should certainly operate for at least 12 hours at any one time.

The length of time it takes to filter a pool depends upon the rate at which the water flows through the filter. This period, known as the turnover, takes between 8 and 16 hours depending on the rating the manufacturer gives to his make of filter. The first period of turnover, however, does not filter all the water. The first turnover cleans $\frac{2}{3}$ of the water, the second and each subsequent one cleans $\frac{2}{3}$ of the remainder until the seventh turnover when 99.9% of the water has been filtered. Fig.5 shows the continuous circulation system and the main components. The equipment should be set on a dry concrete slab and protected from the weather.

There are two main types of filter available and these are discussed more fully in later chapters. The diatomaceous earth type, mentioned above, filters through a candle/plate or cartridge membrane, or septum, at a minimum flow of 2 gallons (9.09 l) per minute per sq ft. This type of filter thoroughly cleanses the water but it needs re-charging after every backwash (see below). The pressure sand filter is perhaps less efficient, but it filters water at a high speed through a sand bed at about 16 gallons (72.7 l) per minute per sq ft. The sand bed does not need re-charging.

When the filter gets dirty, pressure builds up inside it. You should then reverse the flow of the filter and this carries out the waste in 2 to 3 minutes. This process, called backwashing, should be done about once a week.

Both the filter systems mentioned above, though, are fitted with a strainer to catch large debris before it reaches the filter.

When you install a heater, it must be fitted after the water has been filtered, and parallel to the flow, as in Fig.3. Later chapters give details on heaters.

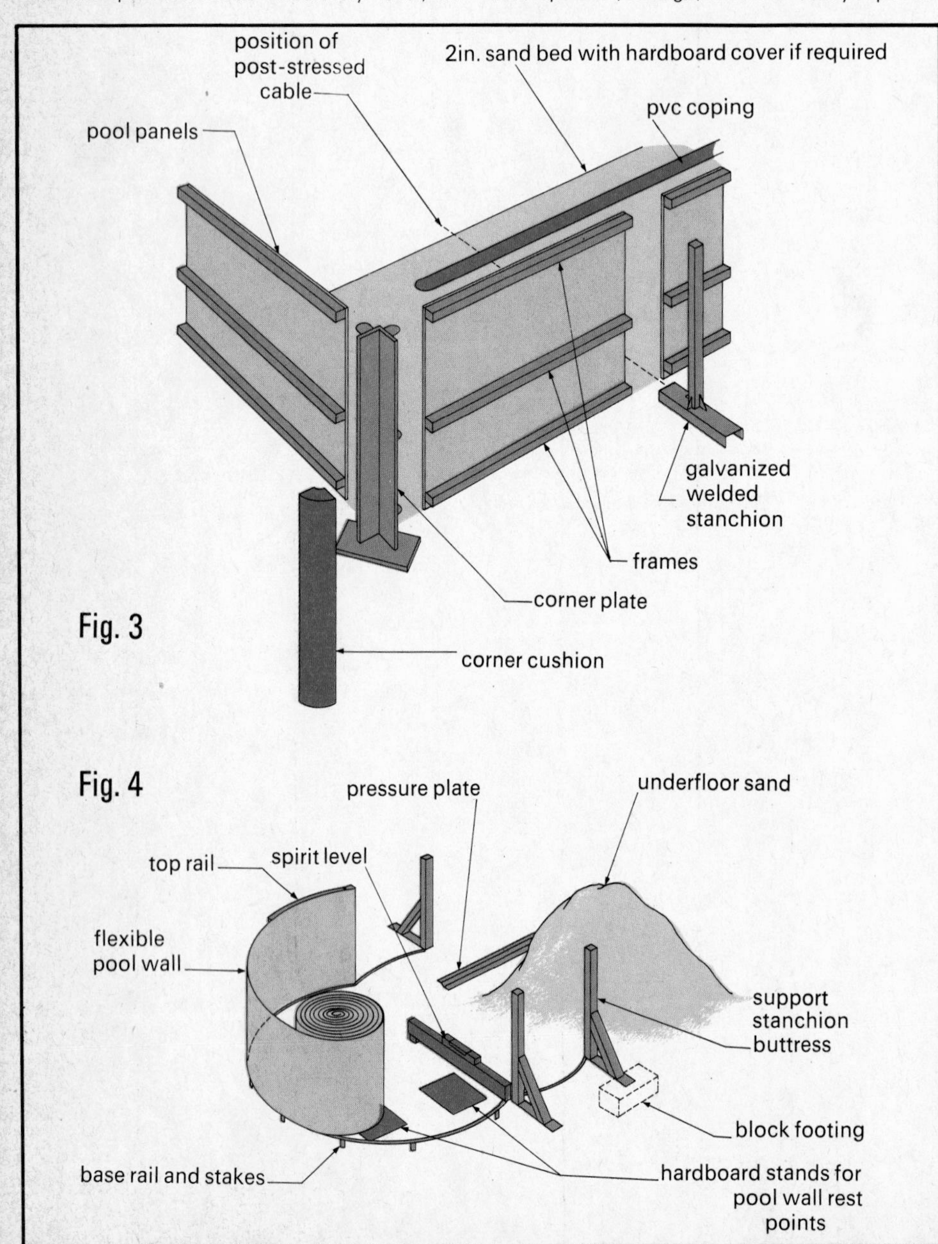

***Fig. 3 (top left).** An exploded view of the assembly of a standard type of pool, showing major constructional components.*
***Fig. 4 (bottom left).** Detail of the building of a pool using flexible walling. It is vital to ensure the base is level, as the pressure of water can cause serious stresses later.*

CRANLEIGH POOLS LTD., CALCOT, READING

Chemical treatment of pools

All pools have to be treated with certain chemicals for reasons of hygiene. Most manufacturers supply materials and information about the treatment of pool water. It is useful to know what the various chemicals are for.

Chlorine is the chemical most used to kill bacteria. You should use enough chlorine—the pool manufacturer will tell you how much you need—to have some left over in the water. There should be a chlorine residual of 0.3 to 0.5 parts per million. It is this residual that goes on killing bacteria that enter the pool after the initial treatment with chlorine. This action causes a process of oxidation to occur—which uses up the chlorine, so it should be replaced regularly.

The water has to be neutralized as it may be acidic or alkaline, hard or soft. The chlorine raises the alkaline level so a control chemical (acid) is added to adjust the acid/alkaline level. This makes the chlorine more effective and prevents the water causing eye irritation. The acid/alkaline content is measured as the pH value and pool water should be alkaline to a pH value of 7.2 to 7.6, 7.0 being neutral.

An algaecide should be added to the pool regularly to control algae such as black spots and green slime. This does not replace chlorination.

A simple water test set is used to measure the chlorine level and the pH adjustments, and the results of the test are compared with standard colour codes supplied by the pool manufacturers. Further details of the chemical treatment of pools are in later chapters.

Fig.5 (below). *A typical circulation system, showing the main components:*
1. Skimmer and strainer fitting.
2. Overwall outlet/hair and lint strainer.
3. Pump and base.
4. Motor with overload protection and stainless steel shaft.
5. Switch and control valve.
6. PVC pipe with drain cock.
7. Filter tank, media, and base.
8. Pressure gauge.
9. Air relief valve.
10. Filter lid.
11. Backwash pipe to waste.
12. Heater, with shut-off valves shown. The heater can be by-passed using these.
13. In-wall inlet.
14. Pool wall.

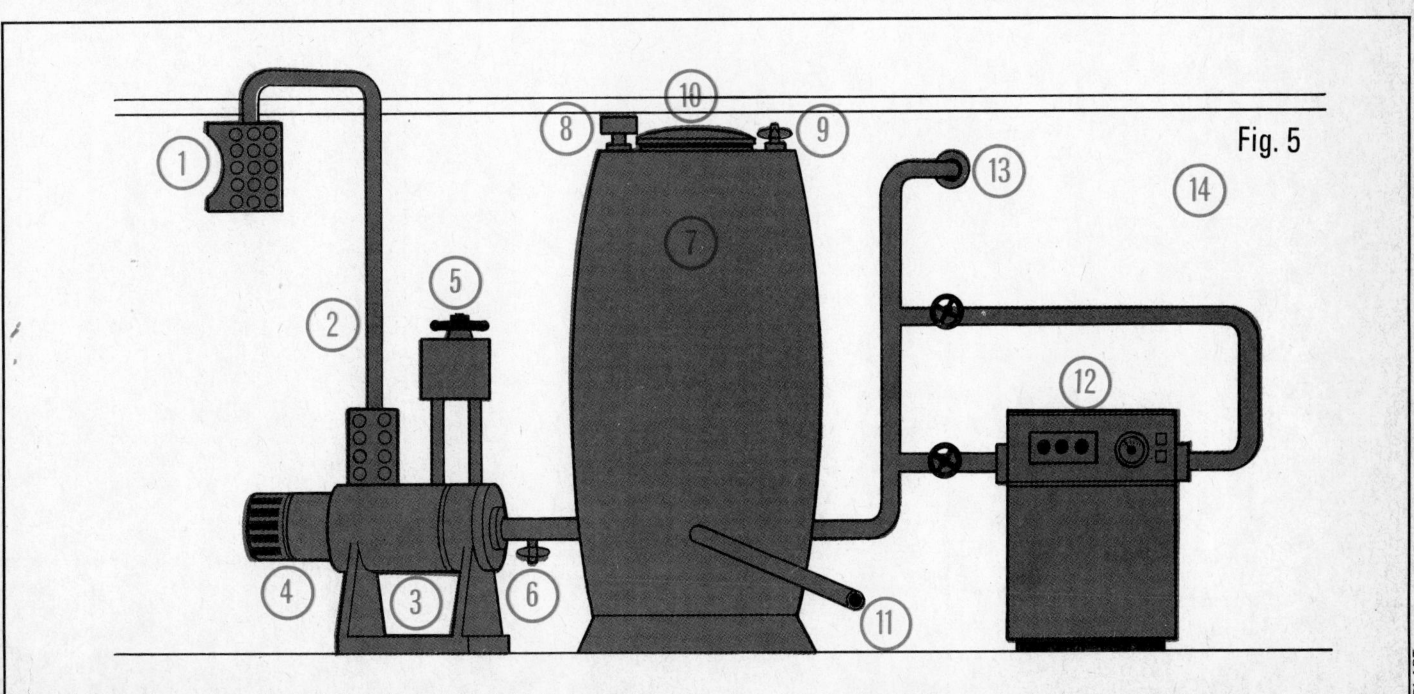

A swimming pool to make: 1

A swimming pool adds enormously to your recreational facilities and to the value of your home. A pool also rapidly becomes a focal point of social activities, where you can entertain your friends and family. To have a pool built by a specialist is expensive but you can build a pool yourself and drastically reduce the cost involved. This four part chapter tells you how to do it right through, from preparing the site to adding the finishing touches, to the landscaping of the finished pool. At the end, you will have a leisure feature your friends will envy.

This project gives you full instructions on how to build a swimming pool of classical design. The pool can be built over a reasonable number of days or over weekends and will look as good as any specialist-built pool—yet will involve less than half the cost.

The structural design is the same as that used by the majority of specialist pool contractors. Local builders can be used to do some sections of the work to speed up the project—as your plans become more detailed you have the choice of saving time or expense. The design and construction of the pool described here is as good as that of any specialist built pool—in fact, some of the better aspects of pool design are included, and alternative ideas which may be more practical in your case.

And the previous chapter, which concentrates on free standing swimming pools, should be read in conjunction with this chapter.

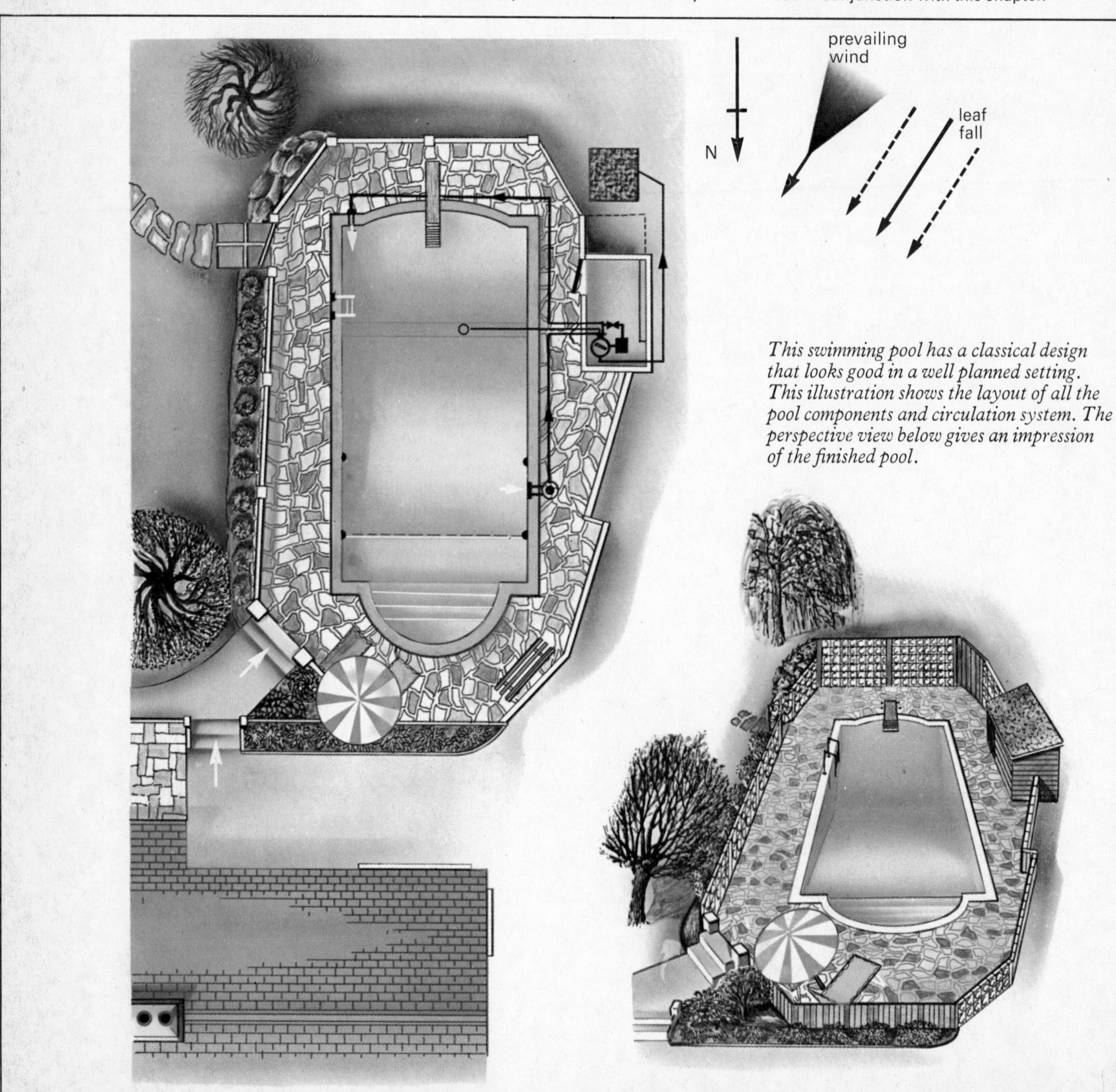

This swimming pool has a classical design that looks good in a well planned setting. This illustration shows the layout of all the pool components and circulation system. The perspective view below gives an impression of the finished pool.

Programme and Schedule

No. of Days	Job/Materials Guide	Quantity
1-2	Site clearance and setting out	
2-4	EXCAVATION	
	Hire of excavator/mixer/barrow/cartage to tip	
5-8	BASE	
	2in. land drains	50ft
	1in.-2in. drainage beach	4 cu yds
	Waterproof paper/polythene	50 sq yds
	Ready-mix blinding screed (if paper not firm enough)	$1\frac{1}{2}$ cu yds
	6in. ready-mix base and 9in. wall foundations	10 cu yds
	alternatively hand mix 4:2:1 (coarse aggregate)	
	$\frac{3}{8}$in. mild steel rod (no rust scale) and walls	3,000 ft
	$\frac{3}{8}$in. mild steel rod starters (3ft 6in. approx.)	150
	alternative 6 lb per sq yd 6in. mesh reinforcement (delete 1,200ft rod)	
10-14	WALLS/BACKFILL	
	18in. x 9in. x 9in. 2-core hollow concrete blocks	330
	$\frac{3}{8}$in. block fill aggregate	4 cu yds
	Sharp sand (clean)—and coping/render	8 cu yds
	Grey cement—and coping/render	50 cwt
	(Block mix 4:2:1)	
	(Building mix 4:1)	
10-12	RENDER/COPING	
	Waterproofing powder (non-staining)	24lbs
	Cement render mix 3:1 (plus waterproofer)	
	Terrazzo render—$\frac{1}{8}$in. marble granules	12 cwt
	—fine marble powder	6 cwt
	—white cement	7 cwt
	(terrazzo mix 5:$2\frac{1}{2}$:3)	
	6in. mosaics tiling band (frost-proof)	45 sq ft
	24in. swimming pool coping edging—straight	54ft
	—5ft radius	14ft
	—17ft 6in. radius	12ft
	—internal corner	4
	—external corner	2
5-10	PAVING } as required	
10-20	LANDSCAPING } as required	
7-10	PLUMBING/EQUIPMENT. Detailed in part 3	
50-80 workdays		

If you are using metric measurements, work from these approximate equivalents of the imperial measurements given above.

1ft equals 0.03m or 305mm, 5ft equals 1.52m or 1525mm
1 sq ft equals 0.09 sq m, 5 sq ft equals 0.45 sq m
1 sq yd equals 0.84 sq m, 5 sq yd equals 4.18 sq m
1 cu yd equals 0.77 cu m, 5 cu yd equals 3.85 cu m
1 cwt equals 50.8 kg, 5 cwt equals 554 kg

Design selection

The most important point to remember is that an 'in-ground' swimming pool is a 'one-off' job which is affected by a variety of factors. These include:

—budget, personal taste and the quality of workmanship.
—siting, main services and facilities for equipment.
—access, nearest tip (for disposal of excavated material) and availability of building materials.
—type of ground, subsoil and weather conditions.
—type of landscape features.
—byelaws and safety requirements.

As long as you consider these factors carefully, building the swimming pool presents no more problems than any other home improvement scheme.

Time factor

You will need at least three months for this project but ideally you should allow yourself six months for the whole project, from the planning stage right through to the final landscaping. A useful work scheme allows two months for the construction of the tank, two months for installing plumbing and equipment, and two months for landscaping. This scheme is based on mainly weekend working. The programme schedule gives greater detail of the time required for the various design and construction steps.

Types of structure

There are a variety of in-ground tank structures. Type A includes concrete, aluminium or steel panels, glassfibre, and gunite (a kind of ferro-cement) structures. Type B includes reinforced concrete, and concrete blocks with marble terrazzo rendering or pvc liner designs.

For type A, excavation for the tank has to be carried out according to the manufacturers' instructions and you may need specialist subcontractors to build the tank. These types of tank are useful where the construction has to be done relatively quickly in hillside or wet areas, or where the pool is irregularly shaped.

The tanks in type B are more suitable if you can only work intermittently on the project because they can be built in stages. You will need formwork for reinforced shuttered concrete tanks and this is usually expensive. These tanks present a further problem because, unless you can cast the whole tank in one go, you will have the difficult problem of making sealing joints between the older and newer concrete. If you can obtain formwork, then you can build a tank with 6in. to 8in. (152mm to 203mm) concrete walls and floors, strengthened with either reinforced steel matting (about 6lbs per sq yd) of $\frac{3}{8}$in. mild steel reinforced rod. Steel suppliers will give further information on reinforcing materials.

The structural design for the pool described in this project will suit almost every site. Where there are special conditions that require a special tank structure though, you should consult a civil or structural engineer. Very special site conditions are listed below and these can be dealt with in a number of ways.

High water table. An empty pool tank, in areas with a high water table such as marshy ground or near to a river bank, will float like a boat. Do not try to build a pool in such an area unless steps have been taken to drain the soil. Land can be drained with special pumps, but these are expensive to hire, so quick construction of the tank is obviously an advantage. Type A structures should be used here, therefore. To prevent the tank floating, provision must be made for an anti-flotation raft (extra weight to hold down and anchor the tank).

Temporary water table. In low lying areas, or areas with a porous sub-soil, you can take the steps outlined above to cope with the special conditions. An alternative is to build a partial out-of-ground pool—this cuts down excavation and construction difficulties. However, if you build a 3ft 6in. (1.07m) deep pool there should not be more than 2ft (0.61mm) of the pool out of the ground or you will have to adjust the reinforcement of the pool. A hydrostatic relief valve, described below, or the pumping of the ground water away to a main drain, will overcome some of the problems associated with this type of soil. If the site is sloping, rainwater causes a problem, but adequate drainage will overcome this.

Unstable or expansive soils. Sand, or sand and water sub-soils, make excavation difficult. The lie of loose soil in the excavated banks makes for considerably more excavation than normal sites. The below floor sub-soil is unstable and a sub-raft and extra reinforcement is needed. Hillside sites on slate, shale or gravel sub-soil areas will impose great forces on a below-ground structure, and extra reinforcing walls may be required. Freezing soil also increases pressure on the pool walls so protection of the tank, and pipes, is required.

***Right.** A simple pool design in a well planned setting. A swimming pool quickly becomes the centre of your social activities.*

Corrosive soils. Soils which contain corrosive materials, such as sulphates, will attack concrete. Here, special admixtures are included in the below-ground concrete, and local suppliers will advise on this.

Unusual sites:

—Do not build on a cliff or hilltop site where soil movement may occur.

—Where digging through bedrock is necessary, pneumatic drills or dynamite have to be used—obviously this is not a job you can do yourself.

—Where a pool will be within 10ft (3.05m) of a building, wall or earth bank the pool will need extra reinforcing structures. Do not add to the weight of the tank floor unless you provide extra and deeper foundations for the building or wall.

Remember that these are very special site conditions which will not apply to 99 out of 100 cases. This project describes a pool built on a normal site—if in any doubt consult an expert pool builder, a civil, structural or soil engineer, the local authority and building and water authorities. You should consult the latter two anyway. Construction of the pool is not difficult or hazardous providing the pool is planned carefully and care is taken in the construction.

Sources of information

There are a variety of sources of information about swimming pools. You should consult your local authority. In Britain you do not normally need planning permission to build a pool, unless it is to be enclosed, but you should check with the local byelaws that there are no restrictions on, or special requirements for, the building of a swimming pool. You should also consult the electricity and water authority for information and advice.

You can usually get lists of specialist pool builders, a range of advisory booklets and construction and filtration standards, from national pool associations. In Britain the association is the Swimming Pool and Allied Trades Association. Pool specialists themselves can help you with literature, design advice and information about specialist equipment.

There are several swimming pool periodicals on the market and these can be obtained through newsagents. And you can get books about swimming pools from your library or bookseller. Concrete trade associations can supply pool construction booklets and address lists for building and equipment supplies. In Britain, the body to get in touch with is the Cement and Concrete Association.

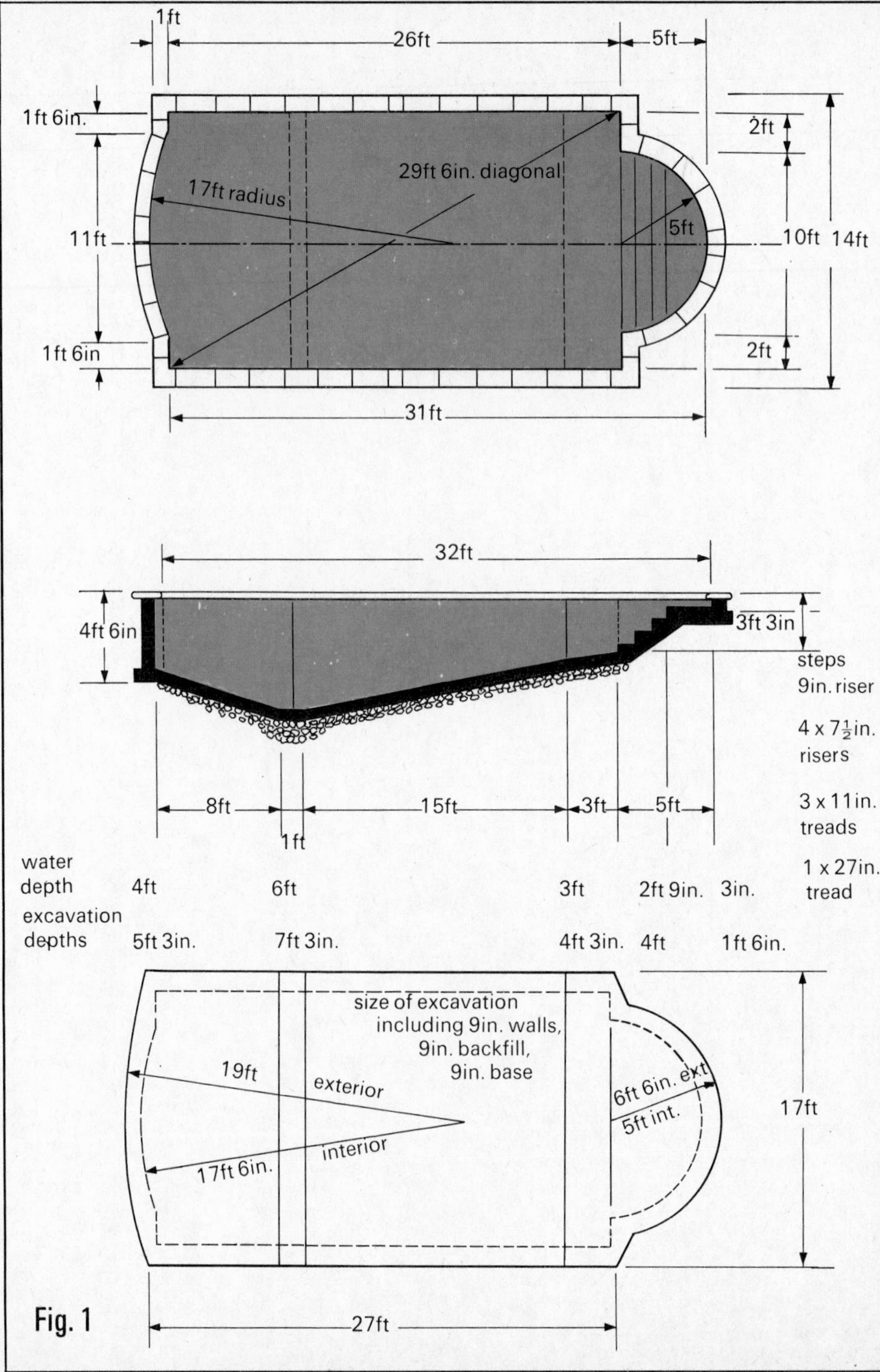

***Fig.1 (top).** A plan view of the pool, showing the overall dimensions. You can, of course, alter the dimensions of the pool to suit your garden and budget. Try to maintain the same proportions though, and don't plan too small a pool—its cost will be high compared to its usefulness.*

***Fig.1 (centre).** A cross section of the pool showing the required levels and the depth of water at different levels.*

***Fig.1 (bottom).** A plan view of the pool showing the radius of each curve.*

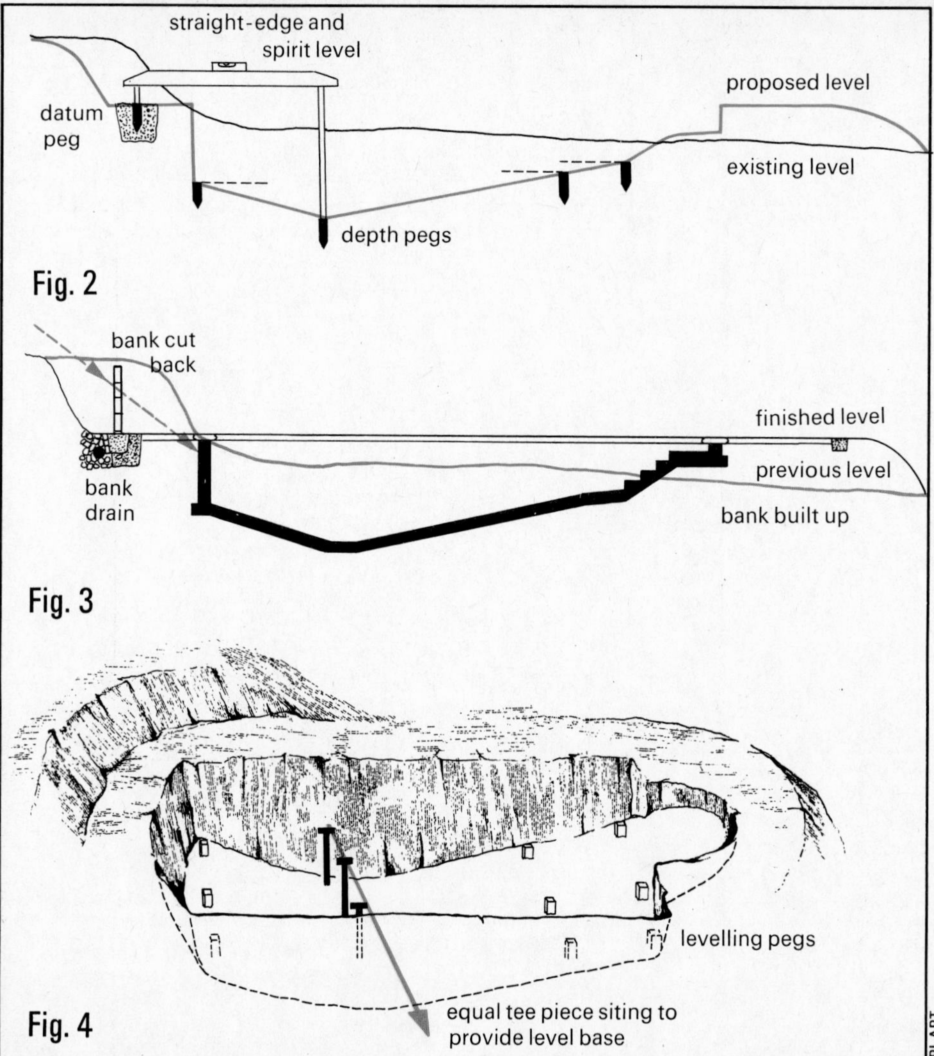

Fig.2. *To set the levels for the excavation of the pool tank, a datum peg is set in concrete near the site, and required levels transferred from it with a straight-edge and spirit level.* ***Fig.3.*** *To dig the hole for the pool tank, you may have to cut back some earth banks and make up other levels. Land drains, at the base of earth banks, will prevent surface water draining into the finished excavation.* ***Fig.4.*** *When the excavation has been made, check floor levels back to the datum peg with three 4ft tee pieces.*

Above. *A swimming pool becomes the focal point of any garden, and adds a new dimension to your family's leisure activities.*

Siting

The size and shape of your garden will obviously influence the siting of your pool. The 32ft x 14ft (9.75m x 4.27m) pool described in this project takes up about 500 sq ft of ground area and you will need at least this much again for an adequate pool surround. The total minimum land area, therefore, is 45ft x 22ft (13.71m x 6.70m).

The reason you need so much space for the pool surround is that most people spend about 75% of their time around the pool rather than in the water. Plan for a complete pool garden, and think of it as another room to your home. It requires satisfactory access both during construction and use, with pleasant surroundings and decor.

If you plan to use mechanical diggers or dumpers for the excavation work you will need to provide an access path at least 8ft (2.44m) wide for them. Remember also that unless you lay some kind of temporary tracking these machines will inevitably damage the existing lawn and paths.

Don't tuck the pool away out of sight; it is likely to fall into disuse if you do. The pool can be screened, but make sure it receives the maximum sun. The area needs some shade but not too much. The pool should be sheltered from cold breezes but away from overhanging trees—otherwise leaf fall will soon cause cleaning problems. Plan for an open space—a lawn or small paved area—for the children to play on. Site the pool so that you can keep an eye on the children from the house when they are in or near the pool.

Plan the siting of the pool very carefully—*you can't move it afterwards.* If you draw up a plan of your garden, and position cut-outs of the pool and other installations on it, you will soon sort out the planning problems. Page 36 outlines the pool described here, laid out in an average size garden.

Setting

If possible utilize the natural lie of the land and plan for the tank to stand some way out of the ground—a maximum of 2ft (0.61m). This will reduce the amount of excavation that has to be undertaken. A slightly raised pool not only cuts construction costs but provides good opportunities for landscaping rockeries, walled gardens, and so on. Tasteful decor adds style to any pool and some useful ideas are given later (see 'Finishing' in the final part of this chapter).

You will often entertain guests around the pool so comfortable seating, lighting, firm paths, colour and warmth are almost essential. Sunbathing and sitting areas should overlook the pool and look onto attractive parts of the garden, a view of your house, or a favourite flower border. Pool surrounds can be as costly in both time and money, as the pool itself and it is often best to regard it as a second project.

If you have children, your pool should have as large a shallow area as possible, with wide steps that they can use with safety. Useful safety features if lots of children will be using the pool, are a fence around the deep end, and a net in the pool separating the deep from the shallow end. You should also be able to see the water area from the house.

You will want a deep end that is deep enough for diving. You can swim in 2ft 6in. (0.76m) of water, dive from the side in 6ft (1.83m), dive from a diving board in 7ft (2.13m) of water and dive from a springboard in 9ft (2.74m) of water. You should also plan for the maximum possible length so that athletic types can have a long swim.

A simple pool shape and setting looks best, and is easier to construct. Don't have too much changes of level (steps and gradients) as they only add to the expense, and not to the effect, of the pool.

Planning

Careful planning of this project pays dividends. A materials list will save you money, and a work plan, by giving incentive dates, should speed up the project. You will also be able to keep a check on the progress of the project.

Arrange for the delivery of materials close to the working site. About 50 tons of waste material will have to be removed and about the same amount of materials and equipment will arrive. Be careful, though, not to store any heavy materials close to the edge of the excavation—this could cause the walls to cave-in. Make sure that clean materials arrive in the right order and also use your oldest stock first.

Setting out

The first step in setting out the swimming pool is to set a solid timber stake into a small quantity of concrete just outside the excavation area. This peg is the datum position and all measurements and levels are taken from it. Remember, when setting this peg, to allow for the above ground protrusion if you are constructing a tank that is partially out-of-ground.

The dimensions given below are for the pool shown in Fig.1. You can, of course, alter the dimensions to suit your needs. Clear the site and temporarily mark out the internal dimensions of the pool with wooden pegs. Check that the pool will be in the right position and of the correct area. Then you can mark out the external dimensions of the pool—these allow for 9in. (299mm) block walls plus 9in. of backfill between the pool walls and sides of the excavation. The measurements also allow for a 9in. floor.

The dimensions for the pool described here are :–

Length and width

	Internal dimensions	External dimensions for excavation
overall length	32ft (9.75m)	35ft (10.66m)
rectangular length (exc. deepend curve)	26ft (7.92m)	27ft (approx) (8.23m)
rectangular width	14ft (4.27m)	17ft (5.18m)
diagonal measurement	29ft 6in. (8.88m)	—
semicircular steps	10ft (3.05m)	13ft (3.69m)

Depth

	Water depth	Overall depth	Excavation depth from datum peg at top paving level
shallow end	2ft 9in. (0.83m)	3ft 3in. (1m)	4ft (1.22m)
maximum	6ft (1.83m)	6ft 6in. (1.98m)	7ft 3in. (2.20m)
deep end	4ft (1.22m)	4ft 6in. (1.37m)	5ft 3in. (1.60m)

Fig.1 gives the pool's dimensions in greater detail. It is a good idea to knock pegs in at the corners and join them with string levels for extra reference (your barbecue patio, Fig 2 can help here). Check diagonals to make sure the marked out area is 'square'. Check the dimensions of the pool, from the datum point, regularly during construction of the pool.

Excavation

An excavating machine will make short work of the hole, it will do the job in a day on normal sites and as such is an almost essential item. Alternatively, two men can dig the hole in about 14 days. An excavator digs with reasonable precision but do not dig the hole too deep as it will be difficult to make up the level satisfactorily, and avoid sinkage of the pool. If it is absolutely necessary, either increase the pool depth or ram hardcore down into the bottom of the hole and cover it with a blinding screed.

The floor of the hole must be firm if it is to take the considerable weight of the water and the pool, so you must dig down until you reach firm, stable sub-soil.

Once you have dug the hole you must set the floor and get the deep end walls up as soon as possible. Weak areas in the walls of the hole and corners should be shored up. Heavy rainfall will ruin an excavation so you should take these steps as soon as you can.

Refer to the datum pegs regularly to check the depths of the excavation and check the final floor levels with three 4ft tee pieces, as shown in Fig.4. You will probably need to do some of the final levelling by hand.

A water table presents problems during excavation. A water table refers to the level below which the rock or soil is saturated with water. Whether or not there is a water table within 7ft of the surface, do not dig in wet weather as you will treble the cost and time involved. You could use pumps to keep a wet site reasonably dry but these are expensive to hire and it is probably best, in these circumstances, to opt for rapid pool construction and the services of an expert pool builder. A moderate water table will fluctuate, so carry out the excavation in dry weather.

Digging a sump near the pool excavation is useful as it can be used to pump water away during construction. If you think there may be a water table, then the hole for the sump will act as a test bore hole. Hydrostatic relief valves (valves which operate under water pressure are sometimes fitted to the main drain of the pool, these allow water to seep into the pool, easing any outside pressure that could create an upwards thrust. These valves only assist in the draining off of water, however, and they are not a solution to the problem of water close to the surface. The valves are only about 1in. (25mm) in diameter so they will not cope with a lot of water and they sometimes stick. Professional pool builders, faced with the problem of a high water table, will design for a concrete subraft, 1ft to 2ft thick, that will anchor the pool tank by countering the upward flotation lift of water in the soil. This solution, though, greatly increases the cost of the project.

You may be able to overcome the problem of a high water table by having the tank partially raised out of the ground. Alternatively, opt for a free-standing, above ground pool, as described in the previous chapter.

After the hole for the tank has been dug, some of the excavated soil can be kept to fill the gap between the pool walls (when they are built) and the walls of the excavation. The top 6in. to 12in. (150mm to 305mm) of good soil may be useful elsewhere in the garden.

While you have the excavating machine on site, dig the service trenches to the plant room (details in part 3 of this chapter) and the backwash drain. The trenches should be about 18in. (457mm) deep and 12in. (305mm) wide with an even fall and rise to the plant room. The plant room itself should be no more than 25ft (7.62m) away from the pool and at the manufacturers' recommended height above or below the water level. This can be up to 3ft (0.91m) above or 6ft (1.83m) below the water level, depending on the pump rating. Try to avoid sharp bends in the trenching—every corner reduces the efficiency of the pump. More details are given in the second part of this chapter.

You could dig the foundations for the plant room and dig the backwash soakaway while you have the excavating machine. You could also simply level the topsoil in another part of the garden.

Once you have dug the hole for the pool tank you can set the tank floor and walls. This is described in the second part of this chapter.

A swimming pool to make: 2

The first part of this chapter described how to plan the task of building a swimming pool and how to make the excavation for the pool tank. Here all the steps involved in reinforcing and building the pool walls and floor are given, together with details of under-pool drainage. The work described here is a big step towards completing the pool.

The finished excavation is probably the most crucial stage in the construction of a swimming pool. Bad weather, particularly heavy rain, can ruin the excavation, so it is important to get the floor and walls of the pool built as soon as possible. If you can't do this job soon after the hole has been dug you may save time and money by having a contractor do it for you. A contractor will take about a week to do the job.

Protecting the excavation

There are several steps you can take to protect the excavation from the weather. On sloping sites you should dig trenches to divert surface water round, rather than into, the excavation. You should also lay temporary land drains around the base of banks of excavated earth. Land drains consist of porous pipes that let water in through their sides and at the joins along the pipework. If possible, install drainage lines running downhill from the deepest point of the excavation.

Other steps you can take are to round the top edge of the excavation—simply hit the earth with the flat of a shovel. Rounded edges crumble less easily than angular ones. Lay polythene sheets over the walls of the excavation to reduce the risk of cave-ins. The sheets will protect the earth walls from the effects of rain water. If you have to delay construction of the walls, take steps to shore up the earth walls at any weak points.

DOUGLAS SIMMONDS

Drainage

There must not be any water trapped underneath the finished pool, so effective drainage beneath the tank is essential. The first thing to do is to see where sub-soil water seeping into the excavation can drain to—this could be a ditch, a main drain or simply along the ground, away from the excavation. This point will, of course, be below the level of the deepest part of the excavation. This type of drainage is a gravity outlet which is described fully in the third part of this chapter.

Land drains beneath the pool should lead to a main drain connected to the gravity outlet, as shown in Fig.2. They should be arranged in a pattern similar to that shown in Fig.1. If a gravity outlet is not practical—where, for example, the bottom of the excavation is below the level of the lowest point of your garden—you can install a hydrostatic relief valve inside the main drain. This will reduce below-ground water pressure. A hydrostatic relief valve is a device with a one way valve that opens when below-ground water pressure rises, letting water into the excavation to be pumped away. When the pool is full, the pressure of pool water will always exceed outside water pressure.

A hydrostatic valve is some protection against an empty pool tank starting to float under the pressure of below-ground water, but it does not solve the problem of a high water table. These valves are limited in size, so they cannot cope with a large volume of water and they sometimes stick. Where there is a high water table, hydrostatic valves are not an alternative to the concrete sub-floor raft that pool contractors would use to prevent flotation of an empty tank.

Lay the land drains end to end in channels scooped out of the floor of the excavation. Make sure they are firmly bedded. Cover the floor area, except about 2ft (610mm) around the perimeter of the hole, with 1in.—2in. (25mm—51mm) pebbles (sometimes called 'beach') to a depth of about 3ft (915mm). Press these down lightly. These pebbles help to drain water from the hole. They are not laid to the edges of the excavation—this allows the walls to be built on a layer of concrete thicker than the floor concrete. This gives the wall its foundations, or footings.

A hydrostatic relief valve can be positioned inside the main drain so that it will be $\frac{3}{4}$in. (19mm) proud of the finished floor. Set it in the drainage pebbles. Alternatively, fit a gravity outlet drain, running downhill, to clear water from the excavation and from the finished pool. This should also be positioned so that it will be about $\frac{3}{4}$in. (19mm) proud of the finished floor.

The main drain is also set about $\frac{3}{4}$in. (19mm)

Left. *The ideal place for a pool is close to the house. This helps make the pool into an 'extra room' where much of your entertaining will be done. You can keep an eye on the children too—a useful safety factor.*
Below. *Simple pool designs are the best choice for the do-it-yourself pool builder.*

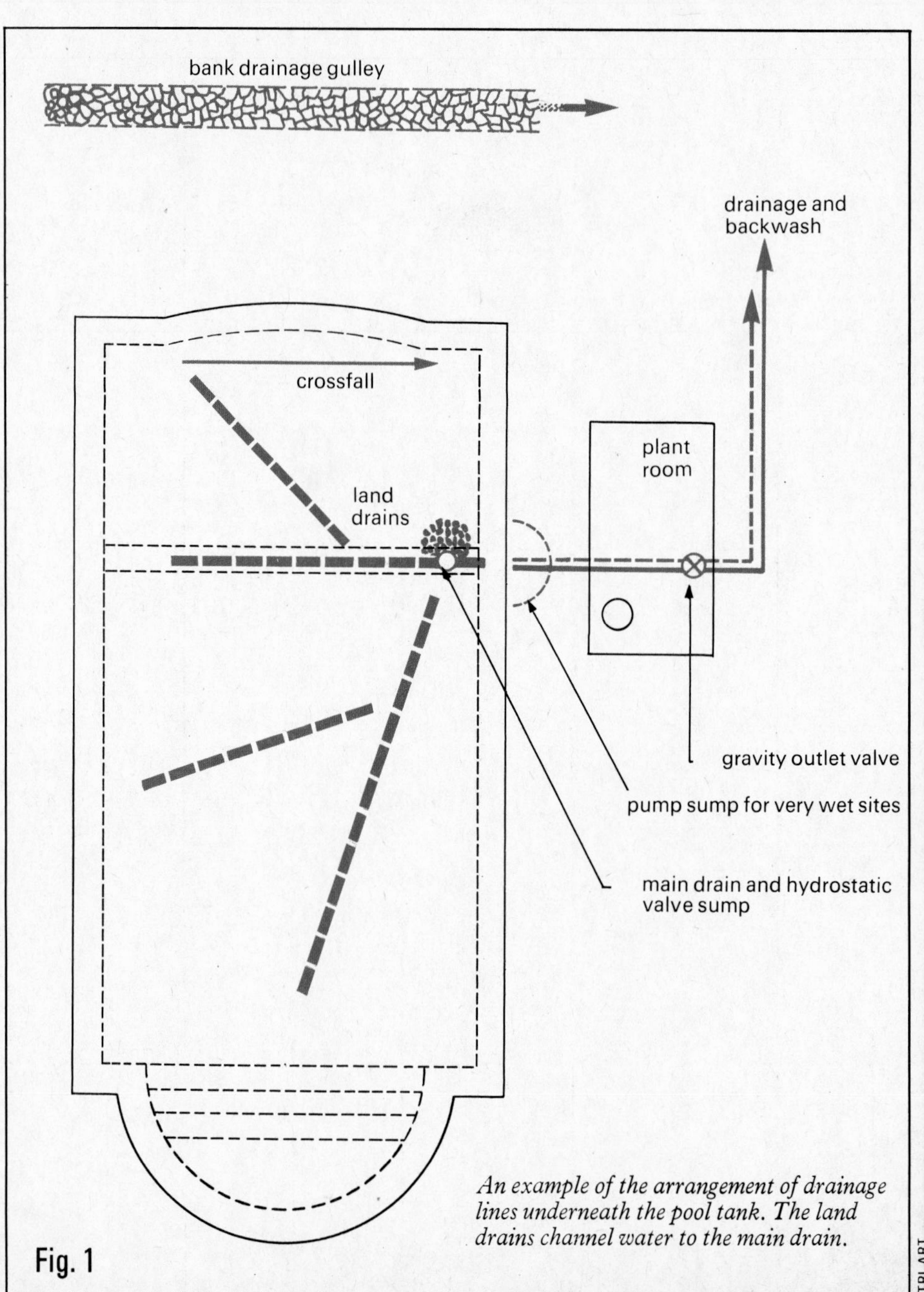

An example of the arrangement of drainage lines underneath the pool tank. The land drains channel water to the main drain.

proud of the finished level of the floor. The suction/up pipe is securely fixed in position with steel rod—used as fixing pins—and wire, ready for connection to the pipework that runs to the filter. All these fittings are discussed in the third part of this chapter and their arrangement is shown in Fig.2. Make sure you plug the ends of pipes and outlets so that they don't become blocked with concrete when you come to lay the floor of the pool.

The next step is to cover the pebbles with 500 gauge polythene sheeting or waterproof paper. Do not, of course, cover the floor fittings. If you can keep this covering, or membrane, clean, you can lay the floor directly onto it. If the covering does get dirty, apply a 1in. (25mm) thick concrete screed over it.

Reinforcement

The concrete walls and floor of the pool must be reinforced with steel. This, of course, is put in place before the walls and floor are built. You can use either $\frac{3}{8}$in. (9.5mm) steel rod for the reinforcement, or steel mesh with a weight of 6.2lbs per sq yd. Mesh is only used where the walls of the pool are cavity walls, the mesh being placed between the two 'skins' of the wall. This makes the whole project more expensive than one using single skin walls, though cavity walls are stronger and non-porous.

The pool described here has walls made of hollow core concrete blocks, reinforced with mild steel rod. The 6in. (150mm) concrete floor is similarly reinforced. Note that the spacings of the reinforcement used in the pool described here are for pools on normal sites, not for pools built in special sites (see the first part of this chapter).

Reinforcement for the pool consists of a 'steel basket skeleton'. The structure described here is suitable for pools in normal sites and caters for a 6ft 6in. (1.98m) depth of water.

Floor reinforcement

The steel rods for the floor reinforcement are arranged in a pattern of squares set at 12in. (305mm) centres. The ends of the rods are overlapped by 15in. (380mm). The rods are positioned on top of $4\frac{1}{2}$in. (114mm) bricks—this ensures that the reinforcement is covered with $1\frac{1}{2}$in. (38mm) of concrete when the 6in. (150mm) floor is laid. You can build the steel framework on top of the waterproof membrane if it has been kept clean—if it has not, cover it with a 1in. (25mm) concrete blinding screed.

Lay the steel rods for the floor in a pattern of squares, on top of the bricks (see Fig.3). At the the edges of the excavation, stop the rods about 2in. (51mm) short of where the pool walls will be. Overlap the rods by 15in. at their ends and bend over the 2in. to 3in. (51mm to 75mm) of each rod to give a stronger reinforcement. Where the rods cross, bind them together with 18 gauge steel wire.

Wall reinforcement

The reinforcement for the walls of the pool is formed with $\frac{3}{8}$in. (9.5mm) steel rod, set at 9in. (229mm) centres up to a pool depth of 4ft (1220mm) and at $4\frac{1}{2}$in. (114mm) centres towards the deep end. The hollow core concrete blocks for the pool walls are placed over these rods.

The wall reinforcement is built up from the base of the walls with 'starter' rods, 3ft to 4ft (915mm to 1220mm) in length. These are bent at 90° in the middle so that part of them rests on the floor and are tied to the floor reinforcement with wire. The wall reinforcement is held away from the sides of the excavation with support pins made from $\frac{3}{8}$in. (9.5mm) rods, hooked over at one end and pushed into the earth wall at the other.

Position the starter rods carefully, remembering to allow for $\frac{1}{2}$in. (13mm) width of mortar joint between the blocks. Bind vertical rods to the starters with 18 gauge wire. Push support pins in place where necessary. Do not position all the deep end rods at once—this will cut down the amount of lifting of the hollow core concrete

Fig.2. *A cross section of the under tank drainage necessary for the pool described in this chapter. The hydrostatic relief valve allows below ground water to seep into the pool tank when it is empty. The water is then pumped away. The valve is used where water cannot be drained to a point in the garden lower than the main drain in the tank floor.*
Fig.3. *Details of the steel reinforcement of the concrete swimming pool tank. The vertical rods in the pool walls are put in place after each course of concrete blocks is laid. The detail (top right) shows the step reinforcement (see Fig.1 in part 1 of this chapter).*

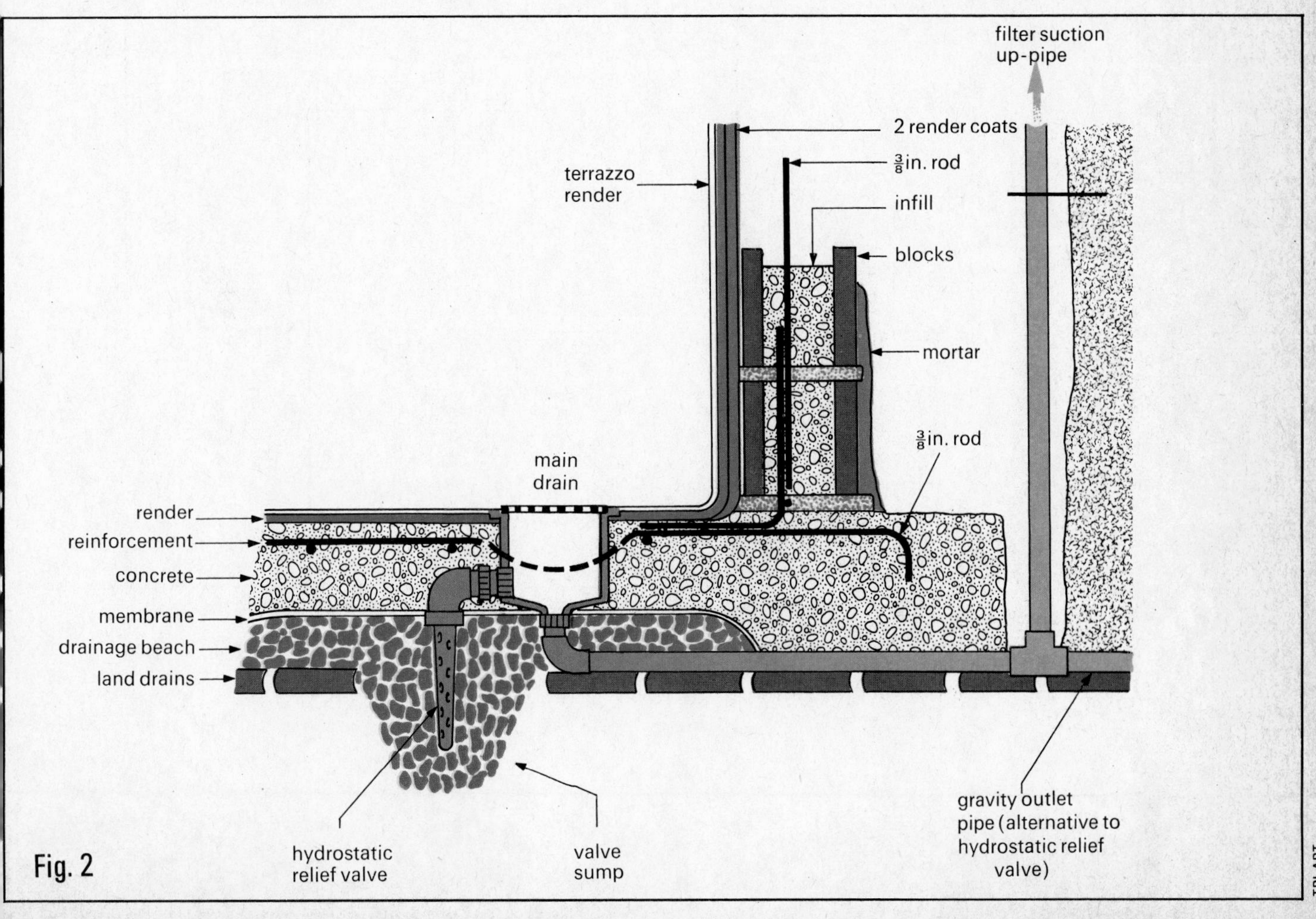

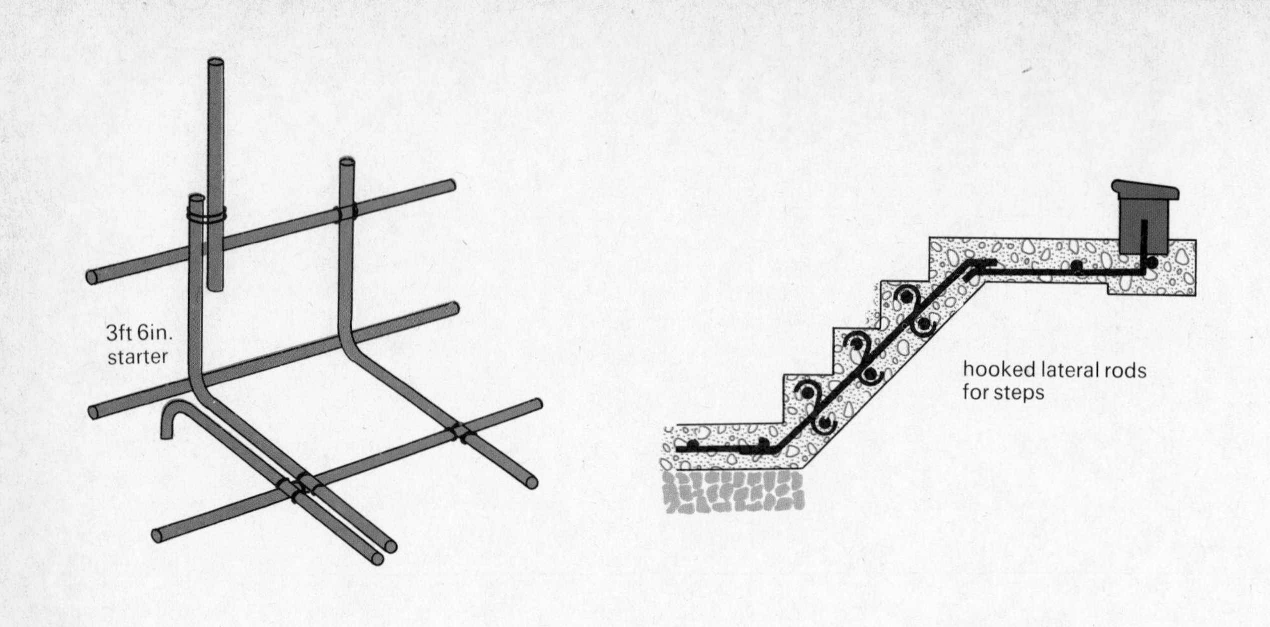
3ft 6in.
starter
hooked lateral rods
for steps

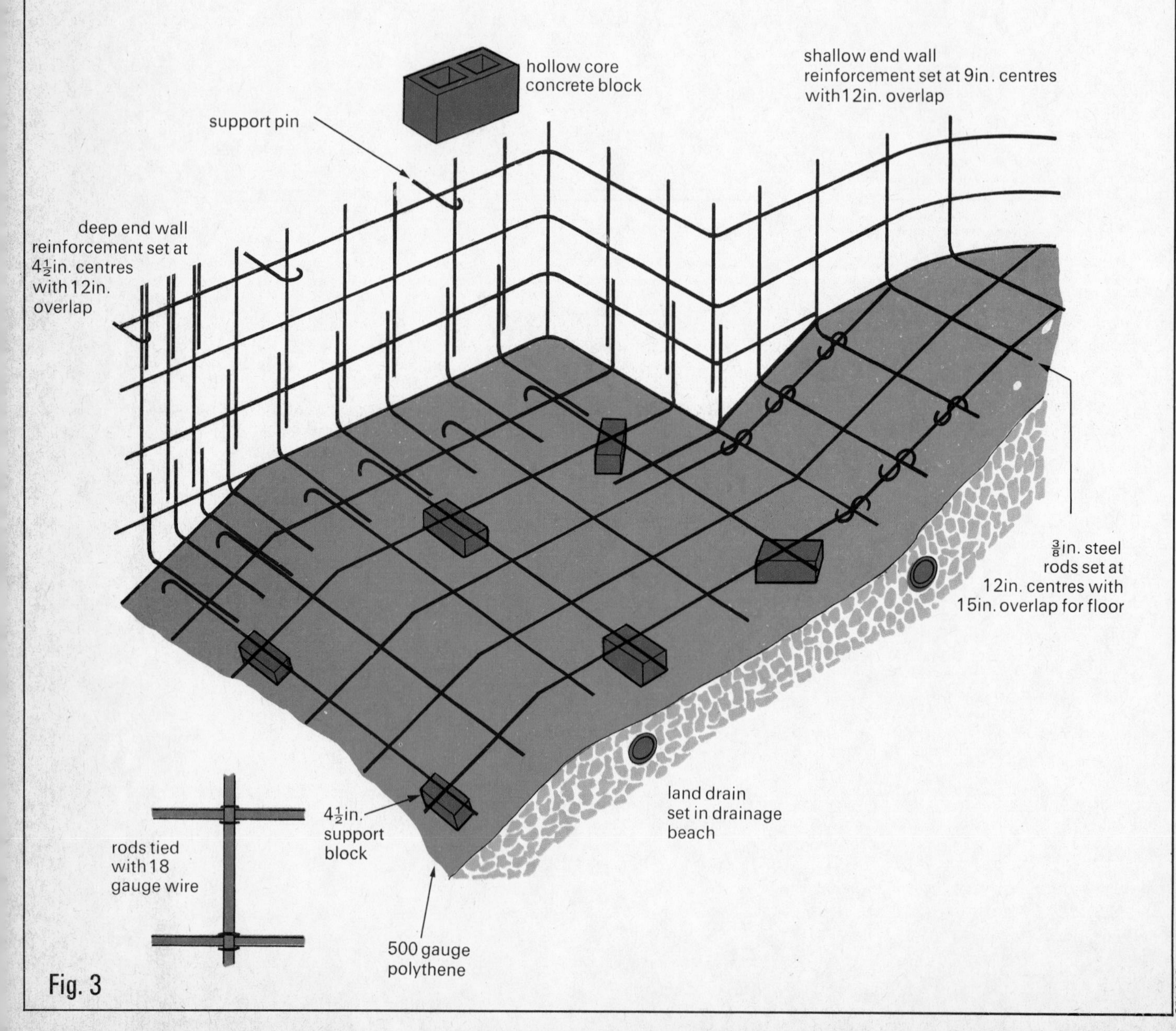
hollow core
concrete block
shallow end wall
reinforcement set at 9in. centres
with 12in. overlap
support pin
deep end wall
reinforcement set at
4½in. centres
with 12in.
overlap
⅜in. steel
rods set at
12in. centres with
15in. overlap for floor
land drain
set in drainage
beach
4½in.
support
block
rods tied
with 18
gauge wire
500 gauge
polythene

Fig. 3

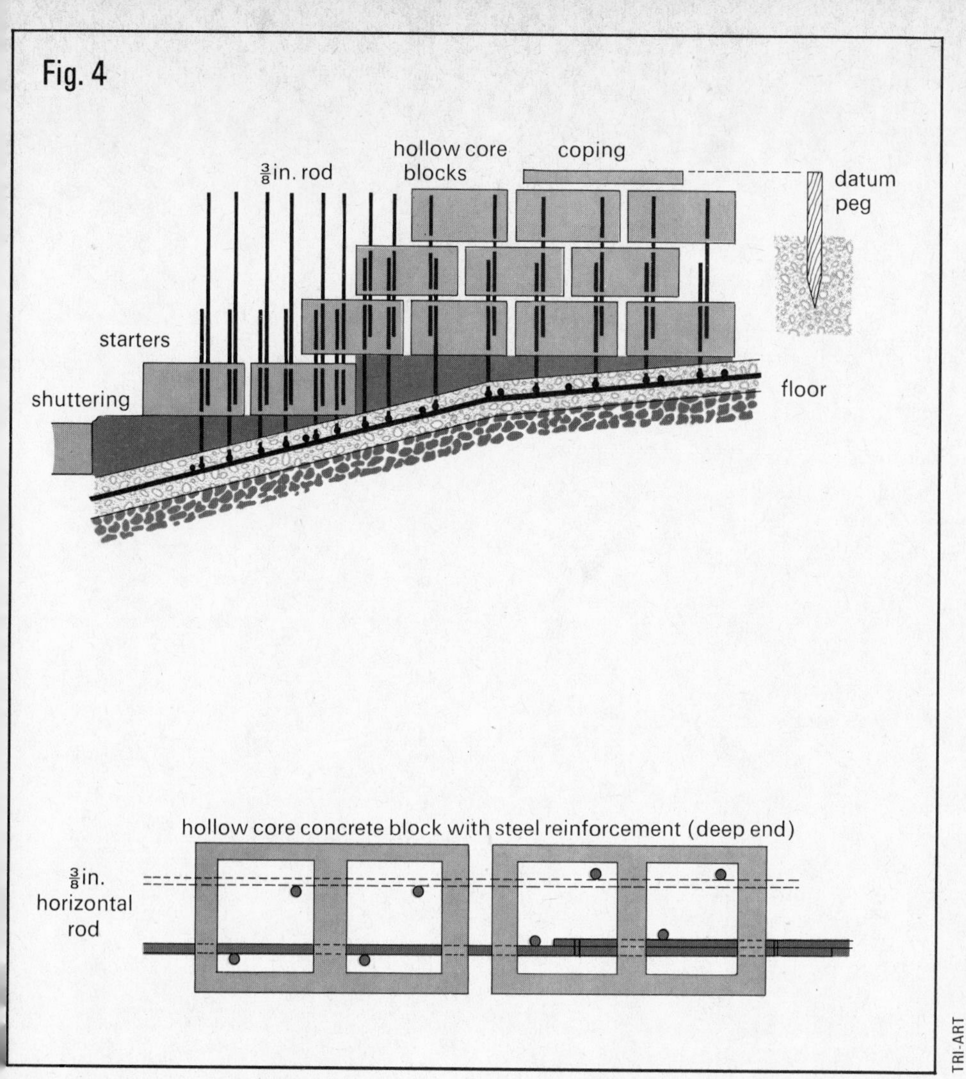

Fig.4. The pool walls, built of hollow core concrete blocks. Make sure that each blockwork course is level by referring back to the datum peg. The lower diagram shows the position of the vertical reinforcing rods, one in opposite corners of each hollow core.

blocks that you will have to do later.

Make sure that all the steel rods used in the reinforcement are free from rust and scale. Also clear any fallen earth from around the steel framework as this will reduce the strength of the concrete that is used later to fill the hollow cores of the wall blocks.

Laying the floor

Use a concrete mix of four parts shingle, two parts sharp sand and one part cement. Working from the shallow end, and taking care not to cover the floor fittings, lay 6in. (150mm) of concrete over the steel reinforcement. Remove the blocks from under the steel rods as you go. Firmly tamp down the concrete to give a dense, coarse finish. Check all levels back to the datum peg (see the first part of this chapter).

There are a few points to remember when doing this job. The whole floor and footings should be laid in the same day so make sure you have sufficient help, and a concrete mixer on site. Use only clean, good quality materials. Do not mix the concrete too wet or it will start to compact, or 'slump', before you lay it. Use just enough water to make the concrete workable.

The newly laid floor will take a week to cure and it should be protected from heat and cold during this period with waterproof coverings. You can use the time to build the formwork for the steps and plan their reinforcement. The steps are shown in Fig.3. You could also lay the concrete for the floor of the equipment room.

Building the walls

The walls of the pool are built up with 18in. x 9in. x 9in. (457mm x 229mm x 229mm) hollow core concrete blocks. They are set on the footings, leaving 9in. (229mm) between the pool walls and the walls of the excavation. The blocks are laid with normal semi-block bond throughout (see Fig.4) and the blocks are bonded at the corners as for brickwork. Steel rods are laid horizontally in the ½in. (13mm) mortar course between each course of blocks—these rods are woven in and out of the vertical rods.

The hollow core concrete blocks are porous so impervious render coats or liners are essential for watertightness. Where there is a water table, the back of the blocks (the side facing the excavation walls) must be covered with a ½in. (13mm) coating of render. This back coat is applied as each brickwork course is built. The render stops water seepage from the surrounding earth lifting off the internal render coat which is applied later.

The incline of the excavation floor is levelled off with concrete set in formwork—this job is done in stages as you proceed with setting the blockwork walls.

It is important that the number of block courses from the finished level datum peg be calculated. Allow for ½in. (13mm) mortar courses between the blocks and 2in. (51mm) for coping (described in part 4 of this chapter). A 6ft 6in. (1.98m) depth of water, therefore, requires 7ft (2.13m) of walling, calculated as follows:

8 x 9in. blocks	equals	6ft
8 x ½in. joints	equals	4in.
1 x 2in. coping	equals	2in.
shuttering concrete to level incline		6in. (deepest point)
		7ft 0in.

This calculation is for the size of block given above. Blocks do vary in size by as much as ¾in. (19mm) depending on the manufacturer, so check the size of the block you are using.

Make sure, before and during the construction of the walls, that the levels and lines are correct. Start the job at the deep and and shutter the sloping floor in the corner to give a level base. Pour concrete into the formwork and set the first block in place, sliding it down over the horizontal reinforcement. Continue this process until the first block course is laid, and then install a horizontal rod, on top of the blocks and woven in and out of the vertical reinforcement. Make sure, when laying the first and subsequent block courses, that the vertical rods are clear of the inner sides of the blocks.

Work towards the shallow end. When the wall is level with the foundation for the end wall at the corner, you can start to build up the blockwork at the corners—this will make an accurate guide for subsequent work.

Half fill the hollow core of the blocks in the first course with a 4:2:1 mix of aggregate, sharp sand and cement. Make sure that the steel rods are covered by at least 1½in. (38mm) of concrete all round. Compact the concrete infill without disturbing the setting of the blocks.

Lay the second course of blocks and half fill them with concrete. The first course is now keyed with the second because of the concrete infill. Lay horizontal steel rod between every course. Half fill the blocks in each course, except the last. Leave only a 1in. (25mm) gap here between the top of the infill and the top of the block—this leaves sufficient space to key the coping to the top course.

Throughout this job check levels back to the datum peg. If your final course is not level this will be very obvious when the pool is filled with water, as the water surface will be perfectly true.

When the blocks have set, push excavated soil into the gap between the back of the blocks and the walls of the excavation, compacting the soil thoroughly. If possible, do this after every second course. Do not backfill the final two courses through—use this gap for laying pipework.

Remember to prevent earth entering the hollow cores of the blocks. Earth in the concrete infill will reduce its strength.

The next step is to install the pool wall fittings.

A swimming pool to make: 3

PROJECT 6

The first two parts of this chapter described how to excavate the hole for the swimming pool tank, and how to build the walls and floor of the pool. This part describes the basic equipment needed to get water into and out of the pool, and how to keep the water clean and comfortably warm.

The basic requirement, in a swimming pool of the kind described here, is a circulation and filtration system that will keep the pool water fresh and clean. You cannot simply fill a pool and then empty it when the water starts to stagnate—this is expensive and many water authorities won't allow you to empty thousands of gallons of water into the drains.

A modern circulation system cleanses pool water continuously. The sort of filtration system you choose depends on your pocket—you can install a simple and cheap filter or a sophisticated system of filtration, sterilization, water balancing and heating.

The circulation system for the pool described here consists of lengths of plastic pipe, running from the main drain and the skimmer weir

(see below) to the filter and heater, and back to the pool, through the inlet. The pump provides the power that draws and pushes water along the pipes.

Circulation fittings

The installation of these fittings will vary according to the type you use, and manufacturers supply setting instructions for their models. A general outline of the pool fittings is useful, though.

The layout of the circulation pipework and fittings—the inlet, filter, pump and skimmer weir—is shown in Fig.1. Before you install these however, fit small lengths of plastic pipework to them at the points where the circulation pipework (see below) has to be connected to the fittings. This makes connection to the pipework easier, especially where fittings are set into the pool wall.

The skimmer weir is a device set at water level, in place of one concrete block (see Fig.2). It is set firmly in reinforced concrete.

The skimmer weir draws surface debris from the pool towards the filter. Larger debris is trapped in a basket within the skimmer—this stops it blocking the pipe lines. A floating flap on the skimmer weir rises and falls with the water level. The skimmer has a lid so that you can remove the basket of debris and on most makes this can be adjusted to the level of the paved pool surround. Skimmers do not clear all the scum from the pool so there should be an area of tiles around the top of the pool to make cleaning easier.

Position the skimmer weir away from the corners of the pool, facing the general direction of the wind. One skimmer is adequate for the pool described here, but larger pools may need two.

The main drain is set at the lowest point of the pool. Water goes down the main drain and along a pipe beneath the pool floor to the filter. This pipe line is called the main suction.

The inlet is the point at which filtered water re-enters the pool. It should be large enough to cope with the flow of water—otherwise water pressure will build up in the pipe. This will put pressure on the filter and impose a greater workload on the pump.

The inlet is set into one wall of the pool, about two block courses down. To make the hole for the inlet, the corners of two adjacent blocks are knocked off during the building of the pool wall. When the inlet is in place the rest of the hole is carefully filled with concrete.

Fig.1 shows the location of these fittings. Since fitting instructions vary, depending on the type of equipment you are using, you should follow the manufacturers' instructions carefully. Remember, when setting the fittings into the wall, to allow for the depth of the internal rendering (see the fourth part of this chapter).

Filter

Fresh tap water can be cloudy and tinged green because of harmless algae, or rusty red because of iron in the water. The depth of the pool water will highlight the discolouration of the water and stain the pool finish. Then, even after the water has been chlorinated and flocculated, fresh contamination occurs. (Flocculation is the addition of a cleansing agent to

Left. *A vertical high speed sand filter—a very efficient water cleansing system. These filters do not need recharging.*
Below. *An attractive and well built pool.*

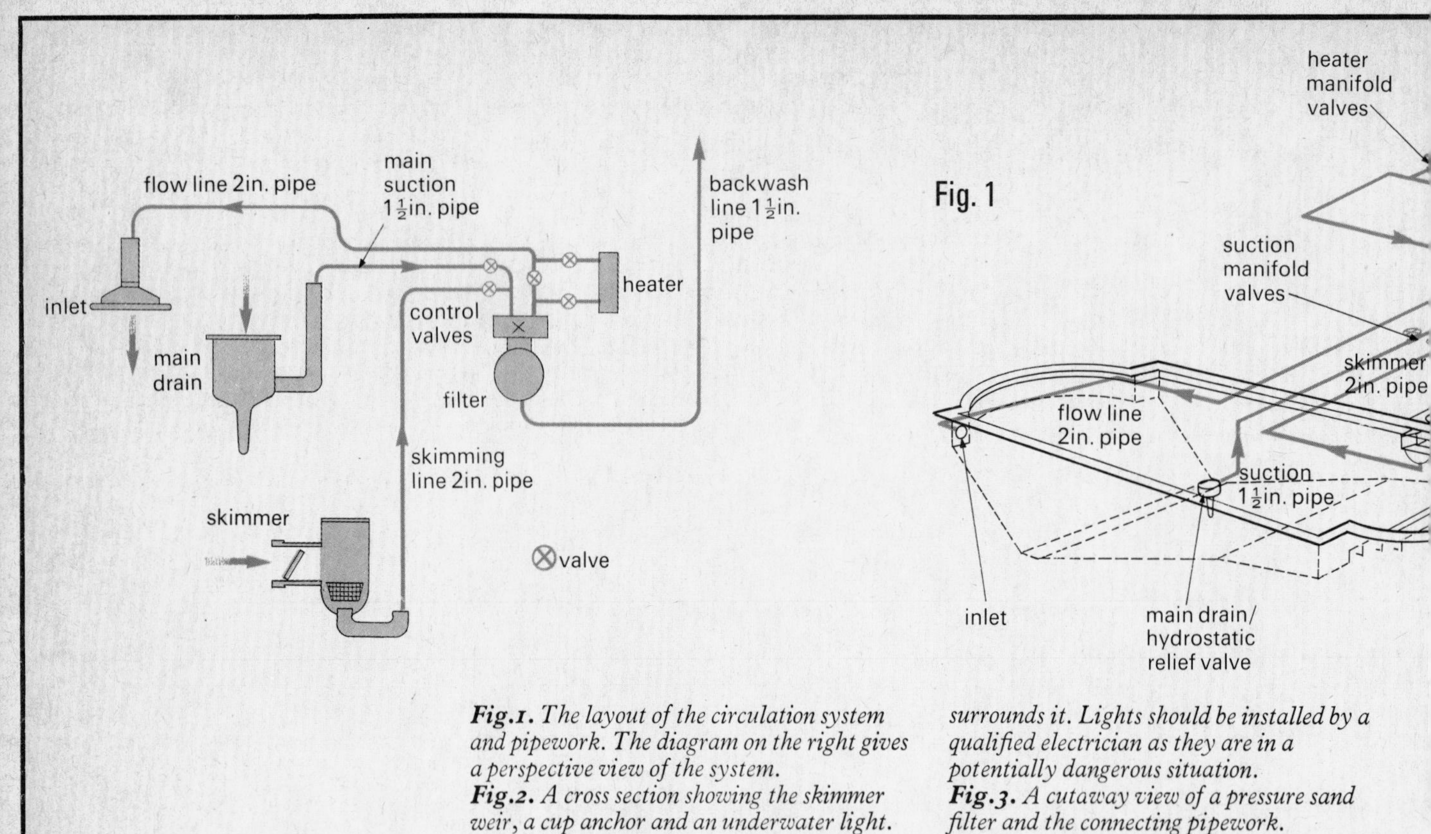

Fig.1. The layout of the circulation system and pipework. The diagram on the right gives a perspective view of the system.
Fig.2. A cross section showing the skimmer weir, a cup anchor and an underwater light. The skimmer weir is set at water level, in place of one hollow core concrete block. The cup anchor gives a fixing for a safety net between the shallow end and the deep end. The sealed light is cooled by the water that surrounds it. Lights should be installed by a qualified electrician as they are in a potentially dangerous situation.
Fig.3. A cutaway view of a pressure sand filter and the connecting pipework.
Fig.4. A typical pool heater. Heaters greatly lengthen the swimming season and are a valuable feature of the circulation system.
Right. *A simpler filter than that shown on page 46, mounted in the plant room.*

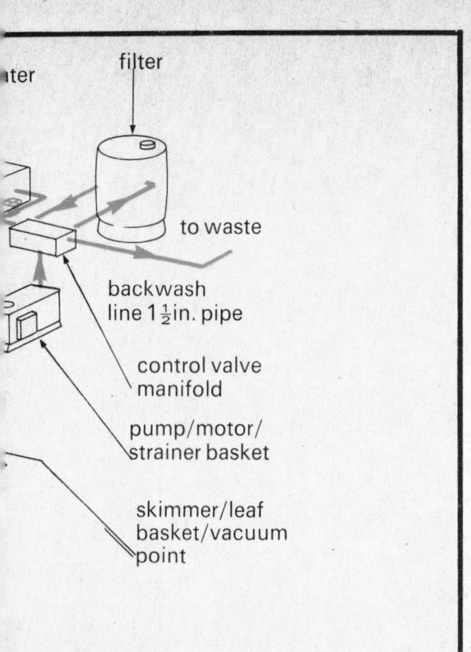

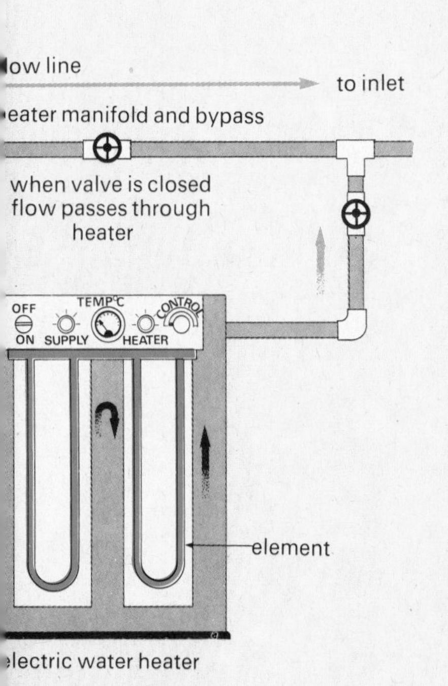

the pool water. This causes dissolved particles to come together, or 'coagulate', and fall to the bottom of the pool where they can be swept away when the pool is empty.) New impurities will enter the pool from the air—dust, insects and leaves—and from the pool users. The water quickly becomes polluted, so an effective filter is essential.

The filter consists of a pre-strainer, a pump, a motor, a flow valve and a filter valve. All the equipment connected with the filter should be non-corrosive. A self-priming pump is the best choice. This type of pump will operate even when placed above the water level and when the main suction pipe, from the main drain, is full of air. The other main type of pump, the non self-priming pump, will not work if any air is present in the main suction pipe.

There are two main types of filter, the pre-coat systems and the pressure sand filter. Of the pre-coat systems, the diatomaceous earth filter is the most common. It consists of a layer of diatoms, microscopic fossilised sea organisms which form a highly porous filter. The pump sucks water through layers of this material. Impurities are trapped in the tiny channels that run through these layers. Other pre-coat systems consist of very fine particles, formed into septums, or membranes.

Water filtered through these systems has a very fine 'polish'—that is, it is crystal clear. All these systems have to be recharged after backwashing (see below).

Pressure sand filters are cheaper than pre-coat systems and they do not have to be recharged. Water is filtered through a layer of special silica sands. These filters are probably the best choice for residential pools though they do not give quite such a good polish to the pool water as pre-coat systems.

Filters are rated by the manufacturer according to the number of gallons of water they can cope with in an hour. The rating should, however, take account of the resistance—from friction, for example—that the pump has to overcome when forcing water through the pipes. This resistance will reduce the amount of water that the pump can push through the filter and so the filter rating is reduced. Make sure than the rating given by the manufacturer takes this into account.

The pool circulation system collects matter which is deposited in the filter. In time the filter starts to block up and pressure inside the system builds up. At a certain point, the filter ceases to work properly and needs cleaning.

Cleaning the filter

Cleaning the filter is done by reversing the flow of water in the filter to 'backwash' collected dirt to waste. This process takes 2 to 5 minutes—40 to 200 gallons can be pumped out in this time. Some filters have to be taken apart for cleaning or recharging (replacing the filter material) but the modern pressure sand filter simply reverses the flow of water to stir up small particles of dirt and carry them away to waste—some filters do this automatically.

The regularity of backwashes depends on how often the pool is used, its siting and the rating of the filter. In summer, once a week is a good average but the frequency also depends on the filter turnover—this is the length of time it takes for the clean filter to draw through all the pool water. For residential pools this usually takes 8 hours but if you can install a filter that does this more quickly the pool will be easier to clean and maintain. Fig.3 shows a typical pressure sand filter and manufacturers provide detailed installation and operating instructions.

The pool described here has a capacity of 11,000 gallons and should have a filter with a rating of 1400 gallons per hour for an 8 hour turnover, or 2200 gallons per hour for a 5 hour turnover. The internal design of the filter should be as simple as possible to give maximum efficiency.

TRI-ART

Pool heating

Warm water makes the swimming season longer and encourages greater use of the pool. If you don't install a heating system along with all the other pool fittings, make allowances for one to be added later. All you need to do is to make sure the plant room (see below) is large enough to take the extra equipment and to install a by-pass valve in the pipe line that carries water back to the pool from the heater. Water can then be channelled through the heater (see Fig.4).

There are several types of pool heater available. The solar heater uses the heat of the sun and transfers this to the water by 'heat exchange'. These systems are expensive to install but cost practically nothing to run. You must, of course, live in an area that receives enough sunlight to keep the solar heater functioning. Oil and gas heaters are also expensive to install but if well maintained the running costs are small. These heaters are quite bulky. Electric heaters are cheap to install and require little maintenance but running costs are high. They are quiet and clean to run though, and the units are compact. They can also take advantage of cheaper, 'off-peak' electricity, where such schemes apply.

Whatever the differences in installation and running costs between the different systems in the short term, the cost tends to equalize over five or six years. The cost of heating a pool in the summer is roughly the same as the cost of central heating in the home.

If you have central heating in your home you can choose another method of heating the pool. A heat exchange unit will tap heat from the domestic system to warm the pool water. This is the most economical form of pool heating. Unless your boiler has an extra capacity equivalent to 100,000 British Thermal Units (btu) per hour though, this system will reduce the amount of heating in the home. Also, if the house boiler is some way from the pool, heat loss will occur along the pipe length.

An electric pool heater should have a capacity of about 1 to 1½ kilowatts for each 1,000 gallons of water. An oil or gas boiler should have a capacity of 7 to 10 btu per hour. The 11,000 gallon pool described here needs either an 18kw electric heater or a 110,000 btu per hour oil or gas boiler. Makers of pool equipment and gas and electricity authorities will give more detailed advice on the size of heater you need, and give installation information.

The heater must give enough heat not only

Above. A pool design similar to the one described in this chapter. The setting is simple, with the plant tubs providing colour and the trees and fence giving shelter from wind.

to heat up the pool in the first place, but also to compensate for heat loss. The initial heating of the water is best done during the spring and the pool will store most of the heat for the rest of the season. Most heat loss occurs at night from the water surface by evaporation and the smallest breeze considerably increases heat loss—one reason why a sheltered and sunny spot is best for a pool. The temperature of the pool water can fall by between 2° to 5°C (3.6°F to 9°F) at night and the heater will have to be switched on for about 4 to 10 hours to make this up. In Britain, a heater that raises pool water temperature by ½°C per hour is usually sufficient to deal with nightly heat loss.

Surface heat loss can be reduced by as much as 50% if you cover the pool surface—thin plastic foam sandwiched between pvc sheeting is an excellent insulator. If there is a water table in your area, heat loss will also occur through the pool walls. This can be prevented by lining the walls with 2in. thick polystyrene insulation sheeting.

Circulation pipework

Pool fittings and pipe lines are arranged to form an enclosed circuit between the pool and the filter. An example layout is shown in Fig.1. The system must, of course, be perfectly watertight, durable and efficient.

Fittings and pipework can either be of stainless steel, chromed metal, gunmetal or plastic. All of these are rust proof. Some waters, though, are acidic or hard—these are harmless to the skin but they cause problems of corrosion to the pipework and fittings. The water, in these cases, must be neutralized. This is described in the final part of this chapter.

Circulation pipework is available in rigid or flexible plastic, copper or galvanized iron—the latter, though, corrodes and this can lead to damage of the pool equipment. Copper pipework is expensive and can corrode as a result of electrolytic action (the chemical decomposition of the copper caused by its reaction with chemicals in the soil or in adjacent pipes of different metals). Plastic pipework is by far the best choice—it is easy to work with and does not corrode.

The plumbing for the pool is as straightforward as household pipework. The pipes used are 1½in. or 2in. (38mm or 51mm) rigid unplasticized pvc or flexible plastic pipes. Plastic pipes can be threaded for jointing but this is a long job and the amount of use you will get out of a die large enough to cut the thread is unlikely to pay for its cost. If you join threaded plastic pipes, the joint can be sealed with bosswhite—a sort of putty made from whiting and linseed oil—but a better alternative is to use thin plastic tape called ptfe (polytetraflurae-thylene). This helps make a really watertight joint.

Sound joints in plastic pipes can also be made with adhesive. Glueing pipes and alternative methods of jointing are relatively easy with plastic tubing.

Manufacturers of plastic pipes will supply full details of their products and directions on how to lay them. The setting out is straightforward (see Fig.1). Try a test joint before working head downwards in a trench. If you are glueing the pipes, wipe the ends with cleansing fluid before using plenty of adhesive—this will set in about a minute depending on the temperature.

Before fixing up the whole pipework system, remember to avoid sharp corners along the length of the pipework, and try to avoid very long runs of pipe. The filter may circulate between 20 and 40 gallons per minute and any restrictions in the pipes will reduce the efficiency of the pump. If the plant room (see below) is situated some distance from the pool, or if the pool is likely to be used by a lot of people, you will need a more powerful pump.

Fit the whole pipework system together dry in a test run, and then use plenty of adhesive to join the pipes. The joints must be sound. You can test the pipes for watertightness after you have allowed the adhesive to set for about 24 hours. Testing the pipes is done by sealing the ends of the pipework and then pumping air into the pipe. The pipe ends are sealed with rubber plugs, one of which has a central hole large enough to take the nozzle of a foot pump. You will need a pump that registers the amount of pressure it is exerting.

Fill the pipes partially full with water—this will reduce the amount of time you have to spend pumping air. Pump air into the pipes for about 5 minutes until the pressure inside the pipes reaches 15lbs per sq in. If the pressure stays at this level for 15 minutes the pipes are perfectly watertight.

The pipes should be laid in trenches in sand or soil—not in stones. The trenches should be deep enough to prevent ground frost affecting the pipes—about 12in. deep in Britain. Ensure that any slopes are even and that there is no air trapped inside the pipes. Avoid putting any pressure on the pipe joints while laying them. The trenches are filled with earth which is compacted carefully—but do not do this job until the mortar joints in the blockwork walls have set completely. If the soil under the pipes is likely to settle do not lay them yet. Lay paving slabs over the top of the trenches to accelerate settlement. Then lay the pipes.

Other fittings

When setting these fittings, be sure to compact the concrete in which they are set—this will prevent leaks. These fittings are shown in Fig.2 and you should follow the manufacturer's instructions carefully.

A *cup anchor* can be set into the wall to provide a fixing for a safety net between the shallow and deep ends.

Underwater lights can also be set into the wall. These operate safely on a low voltage, using a 12 to 24 volt transformer and a wattage of between 200w to 300w. You should get a qualified electrician to do this job, as the placing of the lamps, within water, is potentially dangerous.

The sealed lamp shown in Fig.2 is cooled by the water that surrounds it. A pool light should be positioned to shine away from sitting areas. Remember, when choosing your pool lamp, that one watt will illuminate about 1sq ft of surface water so select a lamp with the capacity to light the whole pool. But bear in mind that turbid water cuts illumination.

The plant room is simply a small shed that houses part of the circulation equipment and pool accessories. Most garden sheds will prove sufficient for this.

The final steps in the construction of the swimming pool are described in the next part of this chapter.

A swimming pool to make: 4

PROJECT 6

The major construction steps involved in building the swimming pool have now been completed, and all the equipment and pipework used in the circulation system has been installed. All that remains is to give a finish to the pool and its surround, and treat the water to give safe and healthy swimming.

The work described in this part of the chapter will always be on view, so good finishing is essential. Bad workmanship or poor quality materials will show at once.

Coping

The tops of the pool walls are finished with coping stones with a 'bull-nose' (rounded top edge) near the interior of the pool. The coping is higher at the edge with the bull-nose, so that surface water drains away from the pool. Reconstituted white Portland stone is used in this project. You should use the best coping you can buy for this job—it is the only part of the blockwork you can see in the finished pool—so it's worth buying the best.

The coping stones are usually 12in. (305mm) wide and between 18in. to 24in. (457mm to 610mm) in length. They are set to overlap the pool interior by 1in. (25mm) for terrazzo rendering or by $\frac{3}{4}$in. (19mm) for painted finishes (see below).

The coping is set on a $\frac{3}{8}$in. to $\frac{1}{2}$in. (9.5mm to 13mm) mortar course, laid on the top course of hollow core concrete blocks. To give a better key, coat the underside of the coping with a concrete sealant or adhesive.

Lay the corner stones first and make sure they are level—these stones act as a guide for the levels of the other stones. Check that the corner stones are level with a long spirit level. Lay the rest of the stones in a series of hops, missing out every alternate stone—this helps you line up and level all the stones. You may have to cut some of the stones. Do this with a rotary power saw with a suitable disc, or with a stonemason's saw. These produce far neater edges on the stones than a bolster chisel. Lastly, set the cut stones in place.

Fill the gaps between the stones with a 2:1 mix of white terrazzo dust and white cement. Smooth off the grouting. If you use coloured stones, mix a coloured admix to the grouting to match it to the stones.

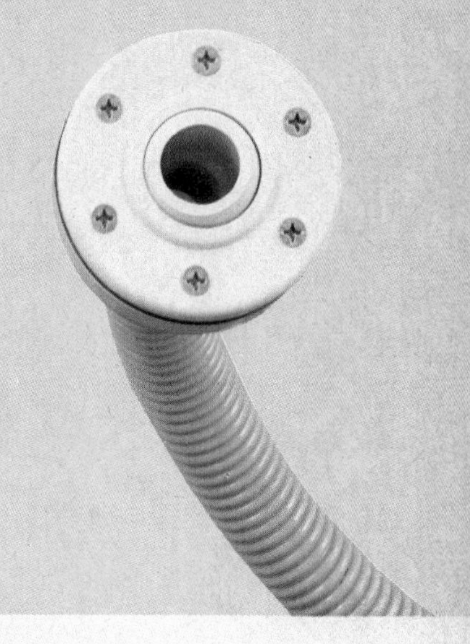

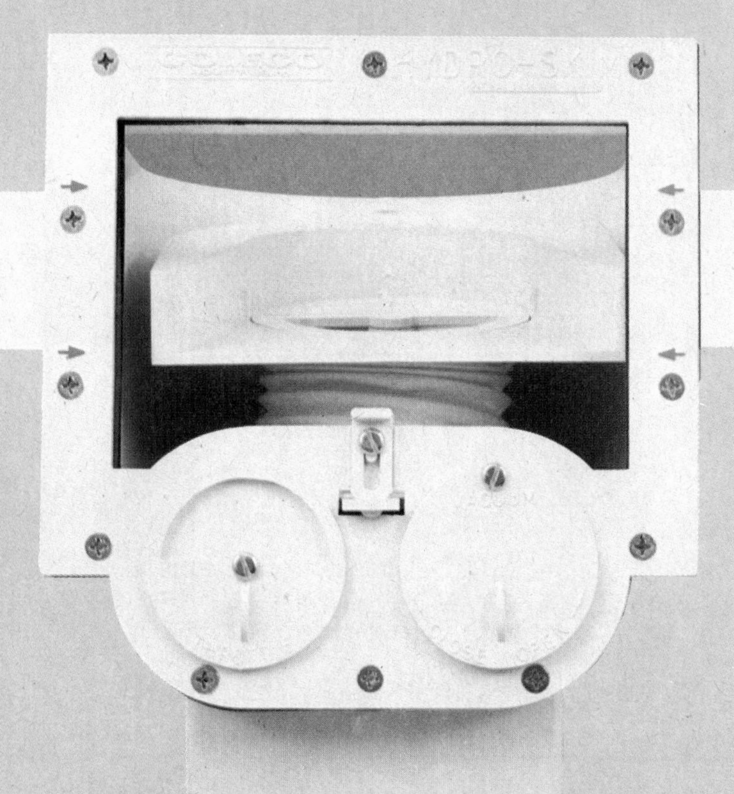

A skimmer weir. Most pools need only one skimmer weir, set in place of one concrete wall block, for the pool described here. The circular disc on the right of the skimmer is for attaching a vacuum cleaner for sweeping the pool walls and floor. The inlet is shown in the top right of the photograph.

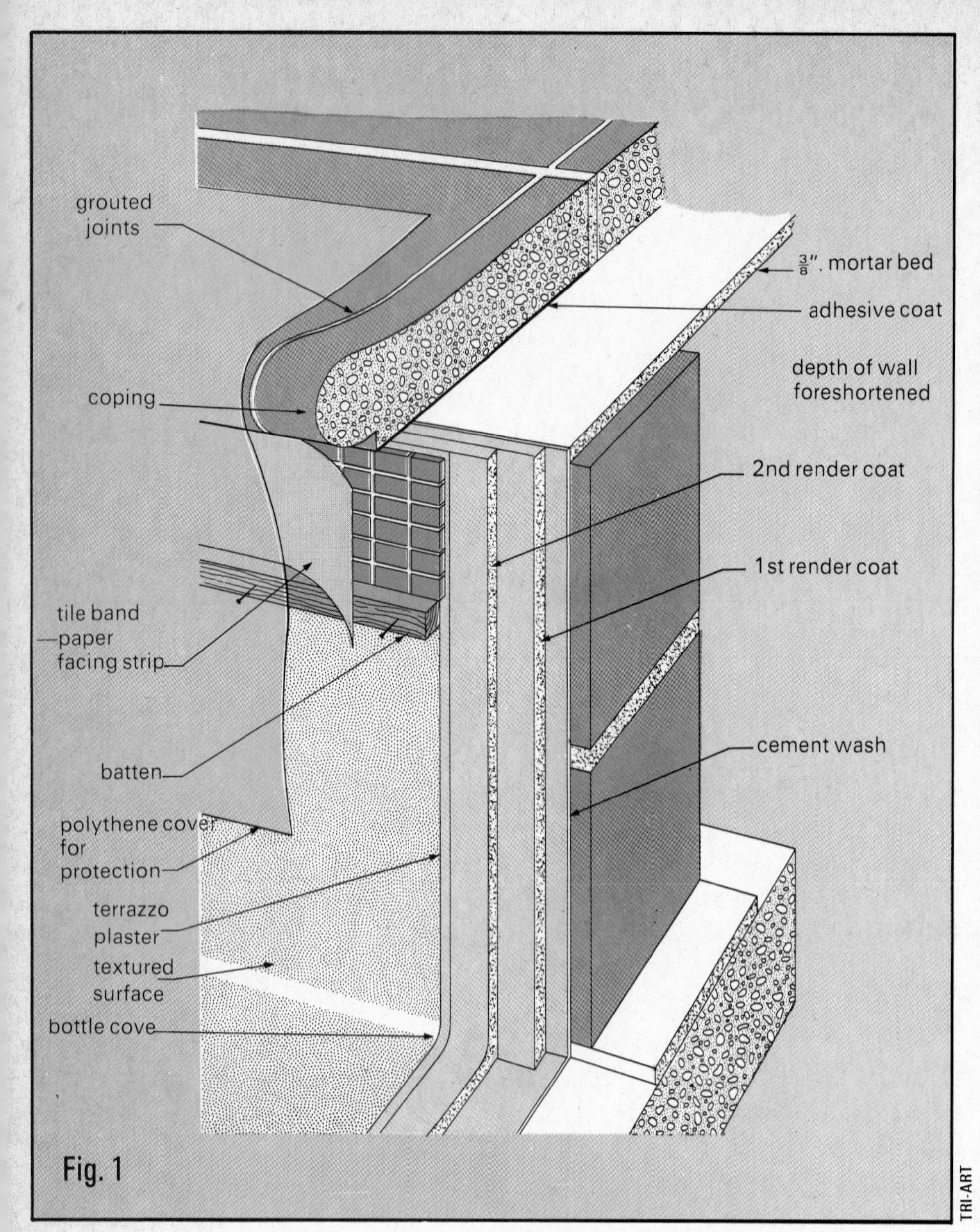

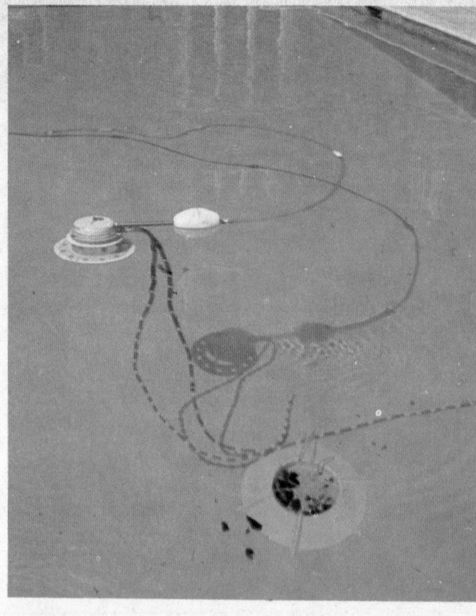

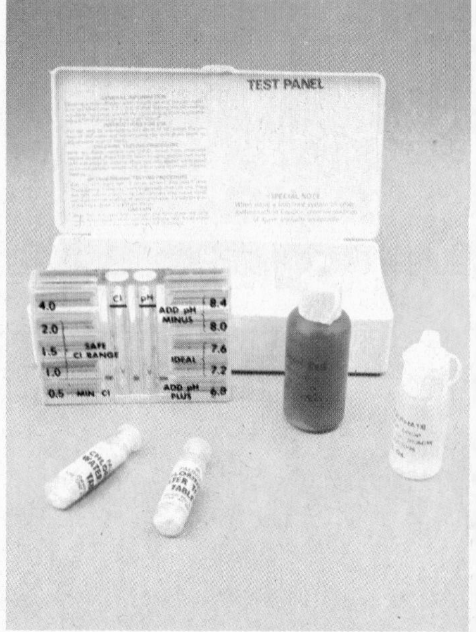

Fig.1. Details of the pool wall lining used in this project. The tops of the walls are finished with 'bull-nose' coping and the walls covered with two coats of cement render and a terrazzo plaster finish. The polythene sheets protect the finish while it cures.

Fig.2. A recent development in pool cleaning, this device moves around the pool and sweeps debris and dirt from the walls and floor and from the water, towards the main drain.
Fig.3. A water test set tells you the acid/ alkaline and the chlorine level of the water.

Cement rendering

The interior of the pool walls, for the pool described here, are covered with two coats of cement rendering, with a waterproof additive, and finished with a thin coat of terrazzo rendering.

Brush down the walls, floor, mortar joints and corners before you start to apply the pool finish. Cover up the fittings and brush a cement wash on to the walls—this is simply cement mixed with water. The cement wash gives a better key to the cement render coats that are applied now.

The next step is to cover the walls with a ⅜in. (9.5mm) thick layer of cement mixed 1:3 with sand. A non-staining waterproofing agent must be added to the cement, as the blocks used for the walls are porous. You can mix a special additive, such as Medusa, in with the cement or use a ready-mixed waterproof cement, such as Aquacrete, Hydracrete or Waterproofed Snowcrete. Apply the render to the walls and to the steps. Scratch the surface of the cement to provide a good key for the next coat.

Now apply a second coat of cement render, again with waterproofer included in the mix. Apply a ⅜in. (9.5mm) thick render coat to the walls and steps and a ½in. (13mm) thick coat to the floor. Then, with a bottle held almost vertically, cove the corners of the wall right down to the floor—do not do this at the steps. Score the surface of this coat with a pointed tool or a rake to provide a good key for the terrazzo render coat.

The floor of the pool is compacted concrete, so you need only apply one coat of waterproofed cement. Use a wooden float when smoothing the cement on to the surfaces—a steel float will produce too smooth a surface.

The tiling band

The next step is to apply the tiling band. This is a tiled surround, about 6in. (152mm) deep, set at water level around the pool walls. This makes for easier cleaning of the pool as the scum line, which forms around water level even in the cleanest pools, can be wiped off easily.

You can either use 6in. (152mm) ceramic tiles for the tiling band, or mosaics—the type fronted with paper that can be peeled off when the mosaics are in place.

The first step is to nail wooden battens around the insides of the pool walls, at the level where the bottom edge of the tiling band will be. The top of the tiling band should be ⅝in. (16mm) down from the coping—do not cover the mortar on which the coping is set.

Mix a small amount of white render to a stiff paste, using a 2:1 mix of terrazzo dust to white cement. Add waterproofer. Don't use too wet a mix or the mosaics or tiles will 'float' and be very difficult to set smoothly. Use frost proof mosaics or tiles for the tiling band.

Apply the render to the wall blocks above the battens and to the back of the mosaics or

Above. *Thoughtful landscaping of the pool area is essential if the pool is to be used to full advantage. A large paved area is necessary for sunbathing, and the honeycomb block wall will cast attractive shadows. Flowers and shrubs in brick planters add a splash of colour.*

tiles. Press them in place and tap them with a wooden float to get them level. If you are using tiles, all you have to do is leave the render to set—this takes two to three hours.

If you are using mosaics, wait for the render to set and then dampen the paper covering the face of the mosaics. Peel off the paper and fill the crevices and joins with white render paste. The same procedure is used for tiles.

Terrazzo rendering

The next step is to apply the terrazzo rendering. This consists of $\frac{3}{16}$in. to $\frac{3}{8}$in. (5mm to 9.5mm) marble chips and terrazzo dust, mixed with white cement. It is sanded to a smooth surface when it has set.

If you are a good plasterer, the application of the cement render coats is straightforward, though time-consuming. You need to have a lot of plastering experience, though, to apply a terrazzo render. If you feel unable to do the job, hire a professional plasterer or consider one of the alternative pool finishes described below.

To apply a terrazzo render, first mix the marble chips and terrazzo dust in a 2:1 proportion. Mix this with white cement, $2\frac{1}{2}$ parts marble chips to 3 parts cement. You do not need to add a waterproofer. Add water to the mix to produce a 'fatty' plaster—one which is workable but not too sloppy.

Apply a $\frac{1}{8}$in. to $\frac{1}{4}$in. (3mm to 6mm) coating of the terrazzo mix to the walls with a wooden float—don't use a steel float as this may leave marks that are difficult to remove. Make joints at the floor line and at corners—do not smooth the mix right round these corners. Do not overtrowel when applying the mix because cuts and marks may show up. If you have cleaned the pool wall properly the white terrazzo will not stain.

Allow the terrazzo coat to set—this takes about 24 hours. Don't leave the coat to set for any longer than this or the smoothing of the finish will take longer than necessary. With a heavy duty, flexible head power tool, fitted with a tungsten carbide disc, clean off any high spots and marks. Do this until the surfaces of the walls are smooth. Do not smooth the floor surface too much as this may make it slippery.

Protect the finish from the weather while it cures. The best way to do this is to drape polythene sheets over the surfaces and then fill the pool. Good protection for the finish during curing prevents hairline cracks appearing.

Alternative interior finishes

Painted finish. Three types of paint can be used for this job—cement based paint, epoxy resins and chlorinated-rubber based paints. These paints vary considerably in price. If you choose this finish, you will have to repaint the surfaces every year with one of the cheaper paints and apply a coat of the more expensive paint every four to five years. The success of painted walls and floor depends a lot on good preparation, the correct application of the paint and regular maintenance. You can get these paints in a variety of colours but remember that deep, clean water has a natural blueness.

Full instructions on the application of these paints are provided by the manufacturers. Paint is easy to apply to clean, dry and textured rendered surfaces. A painted surface does not stain as easily as white terrazzo and you have the choice of several attractive colours.

Liner membranes. PVC pool liners are popular since they are perfectly watertight and can easily be repaired if they become damaged. Manufacturers also guarantee their pool liners (usually for ten years), provide equipment for easy underwater repairs should they be necessary, produce liners with patterned and textured finishes and incorporate ultra violet inhibitors in the plastic to prevent such rays damaging the pvc. The main disadvantage, as far as the pool described here is concerned, is that liners are produced in standard sizes. You can have a liner custom made but this is more expensive.

If you wish to use a pool liner, you will have to re-design the pool excavation—for example, liners are laid on a compacted sand floor, not on concrete. Manufacturers will suggest structural designs for use with their liners, as well as give the precise dimensions to use.

Rigid glassfibre liners can also be installed, again following the manufacturers' instructions for the excavation. These liners, though, are made in large sections or in one piece, so they can be difficult to handle.

Hygiene and maintenance

The job of maintaining a swimming pool is not difficult or expensive. All the pool surround—the coping and the paving—should be washed down and swept periodically. The main task is to maintain the pool equipment and keep the water clean and safe. You should check the heater and filter periodically during the swimming season and once a year, at the end of the season, all minor repairs, reconditioning, painting and greasing should be checked again at the start of the next swimming season. Manufacturers of pool equipment will give plenty of advice on the maintenance of their products.

The real maintenance job is looking after the water. Firstly, the pool must be kept free of debris—if you don't do this regularly the cleaning up job will be considerable. Though the filter removes most of the debris, you should sweep the walls and the floor of the pool about once every two weeks. A vacuum sweeper is useful for this job. This is a suction sweeper that plugs into the skimmer weir (or a vacuum wall point installed in the walls during construction). You will also need a leaf net to scoop up leaves and a stainless steel brush for scrubbing algae from the pool walls. The photograph on page 52 shows a typical skimmer weir in operation.

You must also ensure that the pool water is pure. It has to be chemically treated for this. You can get devices that will do this automatically—these cost about as much as the filter—but the manual methods of pool treatment are straightforward.

The water must be chlorinated to kill bacteria in the pool. A water test set, shown in Fig.3, tells you how much chlorine there is in the water, and the alkaline/acid level, by comparing results of the test with a standard colour code. There should be a residual of about 0.5 parts per million of chlorine in the water. This registers as pink on the test set. The pool water, in this state, is a very mild disinfectant which kills germs. The water should be maintained at this chlorine level.

The measurement of the alkaline/acid level is expressed as pH. Untreated water is either acid or alkaline—for a pool the water must be just slightly alkaline. The job of achieving this is known as 'balancing' the water. The water should be alkaline to a pH level of 7.5 (7.0 is neutral). The water is balanced by adding appropriate chemicals.

If the water is too alkaline an acid is added to balance this. Public swimming pools are adjusted by adding hydrochloric acid but it is safer to use a dry acid mix for a residential pool. There are many proprietary brands available, Alkajust Minus being one of them. If the acid content of the water is too high an alkaline is added. Again there are many proprietary brands of alkaline solution, such as Protek, on the market.

The chlorine treatment kills most algae, but not all. An algicide is added to the pool water periodically to control the algae.

As long as you maintain the correct chlorine residual and pH balance, you will be able to swim in comfort, and there will be no ill-effects to the pool or the equipment. Pools which smell of chlorine and cause your eyes to smart are not properly maintained. Testing and treatment only takes about ten minutes a week.

Accessories around the pool

You can choose from a range of pool accessories. A non-corrosive ladder, anchored to the paving at the deep end, is useful. You could have a diving board—this should be installed over at least 6ft 6in. (1.83m) of water for a board at paving level. The water must be deeper if the board is higher. The board is set on stands fixed onto the paving, and overlapping this by about 18in. (457mm). A slide can be installed at either the deep end or the shallow end. One or two sockets for fitting sunshades can be set into the paving.

A safety net, fixed to cup anchors, and separating the shallow end from the deep end is valuable, especially if young children will be using the pool. You could also have a pool cover—some of these are designed to prevent heat loss from the pool, others to stop foreign matter getting into the water. A pool alarm will tell you if an unauthorized person is using your pool. One model floats on the water and shrieks when the water is disturbed. This is not a good idea, though, if your neighbour's cat should fall into the pool at 3 am!

Hydro devices, set into the pool, make water currents and streams of air bubbles. Underwater lighting can be attractive and you can even buy underwater music systems.

A final important consideration before you start to use your pool: a third party insurance policy will prevent you having to bear the cost of visitors to your home accidentally damaging the pool—or themselves.

Landscaping

Precise details of landscaping around the pool will depend on the size and shape of your garden and your personal taste. A few general points will help you to choose your landscaping.

The entrance to the pool area should be up or down wide steps. This helps focus attention on the pool. A gateway pool entrance—a rustic arch, perhaps—also does this.

Paving around the pool can be random slabs, crazy paving or bricks, or mixtures of these. A textured surface is best for safety. Cobbles look good in areas where you don't have to walk. Paving should slope away from the pool. If the ground around the pool is likely to settle, bed paving on sand for the first year and then set it on a 2in. concrete base.

A sun terrace is virtually a must and you could also install a stone seat. Honeycomb wall blocks will let light in to the paved area and provide attractive three dimensional shapes. Remember that stone absorbs the heat of the sun during the day and releases it during the evening. It is a good idea to use stone around the area where you will do most of your evening entertaining.

Flower beds add colour to a pool surround. Don't have fleshy fruiting plants around the pool though—these will stain the paving. Avoid thorny and prickly plants also, and keep sweet smelling flowers, which attract bees, away from the pool

You could also consider a waterfall rockery, a pool inlet cascade, a pergola (there are many exciting designs available nowadays), a barbecue for pool parties (see earlier chapters for this). The possibilities, in fact, are endless and limited only by your own imagination.

Building a swimming pool takes a lot of time and effort. The effort—and the cost—is more than repaid though by the enormous increase in your leisure facilities that a pool provides.

Left. *Colourful petunias and clematis add an exotic touch to this pool setting. The trellis work 'gateway' in the background help give the impression that the swimming pool is an 'extra room' of your home.*

LESLIE JOHNS

Patio plants and container gardens.

PROJECT 7

A wide diversity of design can be found in plant containers, ranging from the humble clay flower pot to the sophisticated automatically watered plant trough in polystyrene. Containers are invaluable in small gardens of all types.

Types of containers

Plastics and fibre-glass Extruded polystyrene is used for types of plant containers which have speckled or marbled finishes. They have several advantages, compared with clay or stone, as they keep the compost and plants warm, and retain moisture. Also their material is smooth and does not scratch when placed on any surface, and they are weather- and rust-proof. They are light, but fragile and need careful handling. It is better to fill and plant out the container in its permanent position. If it is likely to be necessary to move a long plastic trough after it is filled, it is better to stand it on a piece of wood.

There are numerous different shapes and sizes of plastic pots, ranging from those suitable for containing small shrubs, or a mass of bedding plants, to bulb bowls. Some plastic window boxes or plant troughs are attractively decorated by relief designs.

Fibre-glass is used to make light containers in various permanent colours which need no painting. It is a particularly valuable material because it can be made to simulate lead. Attractive light-weight containers are obtainable at reasonable prices decorated with antique designs, for example square plant containers in the style of the 1550s, King George II period tubs or early eighteenth century Queen Anne-style urns.

Wood, cement and concrete Attractive containers are available in elm, oak, teak and cedarwood. Popular dimensions start from about 60 x 30 x 30cm (24 x 12 x 12in). 'Do-it-yourself' kits are also available.

A mixture of cement and asbestos makes useful containers. While a little heavy, they are durable, frost-resistant and it is easy to drill drainage holes in them. Some are made in unusual shapes. Containers made from this material are useful as water containers for small fountains or waterfalls.

Concrete containers are often ornate. The Tudor- or Italian-style vases 50cm (20ins) high by 45cm (18in) diameter are suitable for very small areas, while Regency-style and informal fluted vases, 1m (3ft) high, look better in relatively larger areas.

Hand-made pots Beautifully designed pots in diverse shapes and sizes are increasing in popularity. Wall pots and deep containers, for trees and shrubs can be bought. One advantage of this type of container is that some potters will make pots to a customer's special design. Drainage is good if hand-made pots are well-crocked, and they can be made frost-proof if filled with good compost.

Self-watering containers The need for frequent watering of container plants can be overcome by using automatic watering containers, which are fitted with a water-filling funnel and visible water-level indicator. Water is supplied continuously by a capillary system. Alternatively there is a self-watering pot system, which usually involves a water reservoir in the double wall of the pot, with wicks in contact with the soil. The latter keep it, and in turn the roots, constantly moist.

Holders or supports The use of wrought-iron stands, etc. for garden display is becoming increasingly popular. These pedestals have a plant container or a platform top for alternative displays. In some designs the height is adjustable; others are made for automatically-watered containers; and there are wall supports for some troughs. Sometimes the design is in scrollwork, which is covered in white plastic. This makes it attractive and weather-proof. A fibre-glass tub with a wrought-iron tripod could be another possible useful purchase.

Inventive ideas

There is no need to spend lavishly on ornamental vases for the garden because with a little ingenuity you will be able to find a variety of containers. Below are a few suggestions.

(a) Old wine barrels, obtained from wine merchants, can be sawn in half and drilled at the bottom. They should be treated with a wood preservative.

(b) Old chimney pots, plain and decorated, obtainable from builders' yards, can be given a concrete base, with drainage holes made by inserting wooden plugs before the concrete has set. The plugs can be knocked out afterwards.

(c) Domestic water tanks of various sizes and shapes. Holes should be drilled in the base.

(d) Old wash coppers, which are often about 1m (3ft) in diameter, make excellent containers. Their rounded bottoms can be flattened by beating out so that they stand more stably. On exposure to weather they acquire a pleasing patina. Cast-iron coppers are not so desirable, because they are difficult to drill for drainage.

(e) Split-cane new potato baskets, obtainable from greengrocers in spring, make useful plant containers for one or two seasons.

(f) Farm sales are sometimes fruitful with, say, cheap feeding troughs, which are acceptable in gardens if they are painted. Disused hay-racks fixed to a wall make unusual garden features. They should be lined with fine mesh wire netting, or perforated polythene, and then filled with soil.

(g) An excellent find is an old wooden wheelbarrow which, drilled at the bottom and filled with compost, makes and excellent moveable container for plants. The wood can either be left in its natural state and treated with transparent preservative, or gaily painted.

(h) Large earthenware rhubarb forcing pots, turned upside down, make lovely pots for plants. There is a hole at the top, which becomes a drainage hole when the pot is inverted.

With a good imagination you will find there is no limit to the possibilities. In towns old baths, hip baths and old-fashioned laundry baskets have been marshalled for growing plants, while in the country plants are often seen enlivening hollowed-out old tree stumps.

Container plants

Many plants will grow in containers, providing they are given one the right size and the correct soil.

Trees and shrubs

Some trees and shrubs are specially suitable for planting in containers. If they grow too large they must be replaced, but with their roots confined many adapt themselves to the conditions and grow comparatively small.

Some of the exquisite Japanese maples, *Acer palmatum*, are particularly suitable for containers, because they are slow-growing and tend to be dwarf.

The spotted laurel, *Aucuba japonica*, with its gold-spotted leaves and red berries is very suitable. With its striking glossy palmate leaves, cream flowers and black berries, there is nothing more dramatic than *Fatsia japonica* which is tough and will withstand dryness for short periods, or exposure to the wind and sun.

Camellias particularly make marvellous early-flowering container plants, with their bright magnificently coloured and shaped blooms. Although appearing delicate, they thrive well in most weather conditions. Camellias should be grown in rich acid to neutral soil, their roots should be kept moist and their leaves sprayed on hot days. Hydrangeas, with their great mop-headed colourful flowers, are also suitable as container plants as long as their roots are never allowed to become dry. They should be placed in semi-shade and watered lavishly.

Evergreens

Deciduous trees and shrubs become bare in winter, so evergreens are more suitable in containers.

Conifers are particularly effective, being dwarf and slow-growing and architectural in outline—either conical, columnar, globular or prostrate. Being wind resistant they are liable to be blown over, so put them in heavy broad-based tubs. A good layer of drainage pebbles helps to stabilize them. Because they shed their foliage gradually, they do not signal ill-health or dryness immediately. For this reason it is important to keep young plants well-watered. Give their foliage a thorough spray with clean water when the weather is hot. Adding peat to their soil helps retain moisture and renders the soil slightly acid, which the majority of conifers prefer.

Bulb flowers and climbers

Bulb flowers suitable for growing in containers include all the normal spring flowering kinds, such as hyacinths, narcissi and tulips. Choose sorts which do not grow too tall, otherwise strong winds will damage them. Beautifully coloured, summer-flowering, scented lilies are in pots, but they must be staked.

Among the annual climbers suitable for growing in containers is the blue morning glory (*Ipomoea*). The purple *Cobaea scandens* which is usually treated as an annual, will grow successfully too, if given a warm position. Hardwood climbers are also very successful and effective if kept well-watered. Growing in a restricted space, vigorous ones will not grow to their full extent. Suitable climbers for pot culture are Virginia creeper, gold- and ivory-splashed ivies, honeysuckles, *Euonymous fortunei* (for low supports) and roses.

A seasonal guide to container gardening

As container gardening depends a great deal on climate, and container plants thrive in different conditions from other plants, a season by season guide to caring for them is given here. However do remember that container plants, like those grown in the earth are subject to all the same kinds of pests and diseases and need to be carefully looked at from time to time and checked for damage from parasites and other features caused by lack of light or overwatering.

Winter

Winter is a period for repair, renovation and renewal. All areas should be kept swept clean of dead leaves, etc., because they harbour pests and disease spores. A check must be made that the drainage holes of containers are not choked with rubbish or fine soil washed in them by summer rain. Excess water from winter snow, frosts and rain is likely to freeze if it cannot flow away freely. The roots are then likely to be starved of water and the plants might die or the container become cracked.

It is also important to see that water drains quickly from the floor on which the pots are standing, because plants and containers can be seriously damaged by contact with too much water. It is important, therefore, to see that all containers are standing off the floor.

Make sure too that the supports of climbers, straining wires or trellis-work, are securely fixed to walls and also that last year's dead growth is removed, because its weightiness might cause damage if blown down by high winds.

One of the principal aims of a container gardener during the winter should be to protect the plants against frost by keeping the surroundings slightly above freezing. This can, of course, be done by installing soil warming or under floor heating, etc. Such devices, however, use a lot of electricity, and are expensive to install.

To keep plants as warm as possible place containers in sheltered positions and protect with sacking or straw, but make sure that rain is accessible to the plants, otherwise they will dry out. A light soil mixture helps drainage and prevents soil freezing. Scraping away the top 5cm (2in) of soil and replacing it with peat also helps to keep the soil warmer. If a root ball becomes frozen let it thaw out naturally in a sheltered place, or take it to a shed or cold greenhouse, if you have one.

Winter is the season during which you should renew your plants and plant up new containers. If your containers are over 30cm (1ft) deep, permanent plants can be underplanted with spring bulbs. Because of their lightness and water-retaining property, soil-less composts are useful for container gardening, but they have the disadvantage of blowing about in the summer breezes. This can be overcome by incorporating some heavier soil with them or top-dressing with about 2.5cm (1 in) of shingle.

Spring

Plants in containers, because they are a little warmer, are usually a little more advanced than those in the open ground. All danger of frost will not have passed by spring, however, so do not be tempted to put out tender plants.

Colourful annuals and other plants for window boxes and troughs can be raised from seed. It is not necessary to have a greenhouse for this purpose as many seeds will germinate in your house. They should be sown in pots or boxes and then placed in a polythene bag. The latter should be inflated and closed tightly with a rubber band. The warmth and humidity will soon cause germination. Examine it daily for condensation. If high, remove the seed container, turn the bag inside out and put it back. Keep the seeds in a warm place such as the airing cupboard at first. Put them on a window sill later to give them good light but less warmth. Harden them off by putting them outdoors on a warm day when the seedlings are larger.

Many seeds can be sown directly in containers in early spring. If this is done, growth should be hastened by covering them with a sheet of glass weighed down with a stone, which will prevent it being blown off by the wind. Cuttings incidentally can be rooted similarly. It is better, however, to plant some containers out permanently with dwarf shrubs, conifers and rock plants to give instant results. Remaining containers can be filled with annuals raised from seed in late spring.

It is important to clear out spring bulbs as soon as the flowers fade so that they do not look untidy when they die down in their containers. Put them in a box of peat or soil, or in a garden.

You should water newly-sown seeds and plants constantly from early spring. You may find that with a comparatively dry compost, the first good watering drains away quickly leaving the roots relatively dry, so the first thorough watering should be followed by another. As growth becomes evident feed with a liquid or granular fertilizer. At first use less than the recommended dose. Make sure that the soil is thoroughly wet before feeding.

Your aim in spring should be to have all the preparation and planting complete to ensure colourful containers later and to have all wall surfaces prepared to house the climbers that are busily producing new growth.

Summer

The pleasures of patio, roof gardens and balconies can be fully enjoyed during the summer. Seeds of annuals can be sown in pots to give vivid colour later in the season, e.g. alyssum, candytuft, nigellas, mignonette, virginian stocks, pansies, arabis and others.

Low-growing plants can be planted at the base of trees, shrubs and taller plants already in containers. During warm summer days and evenings container plants are at their best. Boxes of flowers in bloom can be bought from garden centres and planted out to give an instant blaze of colour. To help you choose, here is a selection of flowering plants.

White: alyssum, begonia, daisy, candytuft, dianthus, echium, eschscholzia, forget-me-not, gazania, linaria, lobelia, pansy, petunia, *Phlox drummondii,* polyanthus and verbena.

Yellow: eschscholzia, gazania, limnanthes, nasturtium, nemesia, pansy, polyanthus, *Tagetes signata* and wallflower.

Red: anagallis, begonia, *Dianthus sinensis,* nasturtium, nemesia, petunia, *Phlox drummondii,* polyanthus and portulaca *Silene pendula,* verbena and wallflower.

Blue: anagallis, anchusa, forget-me-not, lobelia, nemesia, nemophila, pansy, petunia, phacelia, polyanthus, verbena and viscaria.

Choose plants that have moist roots, which are disease and insect free, and ones that have small buds, rather than flowers, (as this tends to mean that the plants are starved or sown too early). Keep them in the cool until you can plant them. Prepare your containers using a mixture of 7 parts by volume loam, 3 parts peat and 2 parts dry coarse sand with a little added fertilizer, or a proprietary no-soil mixture. The containers should be as large as possible so that they can hold a considerable quantity of soil, which retains moisture. An extra addition of peat will enhance this property.

Water the boxes before planting and lift each plant out with a good ball. Plant with a trowel, spreading the roots and firm in. Water again and shade the newly-planted container for two days. When they are growing well look out for disease daily, dead-head to ensure continuity of blooming and replace any plant that dies.

All container plants must have water always available at their roots. This ensures that they can draw up vital moisture lost by transpiration and absorb the nutrients in the water. Watering

twice a day is not too lavish during hot weather. To minimize loss by evaporation, it is helpful if the plants can be given shade for some time each day.

When watering, the soil must become completely soaked. Water should issue freely through the drainage holes. Watering must be done gently and repeatedly, if necessary until the soil is thoroughly wet.

Transpiration is slowed if the foliage is thoroughly wet, so the plant must be drenched. A humid atmosphere can be created by flooding the floor. If you do this on a balcony make sure that it will not be a nuisance to the neighbours. Watering is best done in the early morning or late afternoon, so that the loss by evaporation is at a minimum and the plants have some hours to absorb the water. Sprinkler systems are not very suitable for containers in small spaces, because they are not sufficiently concentrated and can be a nuisance to your neighbours. Sometimes, however, it is possible to work such equipment at low level and water various areas for an hour at a time.

Drainage holes should always be kept clear, not only to ensure a good flow of water, but also to draw air through from the atmosphere.

Autumn

During this season the container gardener should make the most of evergreens, and the few shrubs and trees that will survive the snow and frost. Evergreens can have gold, silver, grey and blue, as well as green, foliage.

Dwarf and slow-growing conifers are particularly valuable in this season, not only for their colour, but also for their shapes which look delightful silhouetted against mist or snow. The tiniest are excellent for window boxes. *Juniperus communis* 'Compressa' is a blue-green pillar, only 60cm (2ft) tall; spreading *J. procumbens* 'Nana' is no more than a few centimetres (inches) high; *Chamaecyparis lawsoniana* 'Minima Aurea' is cone-shaped with elegant twisted golden foliage; cushion-shaped *C. obtusa* 'Pygmaea' has fanning foliage, turning red at the tips in winter; and *C. thyoides* 'Andelyensis' turns almost plum-coloured.

If you plant heathers or ericas, their existing flowers will persist during snowy weather, though new flowers will not open until after the thaw. In some areas with hard winter *E. Carnea* does not bloom until spring and true heather (*Calluna*) will never bloom in winter. Heathers should be planted in acid soil, although *Erica carnea* cultivars will tolerate a little lime. Some cultivars have brilliantly coloured foliage—rich tints of gold and red that make them look as colourful as flowers. They mix effectively with dwarf conifers and grow well in tubs.

During autumn plant camellias or rhododendrons which will last into winter. The former are hardy, have beautiful leaves and some sorts flower in early winter—*Camellia japonica* 'Nobilissima' and *C. x williamsii* for example. Newly planted camellias should be protected from frost with peat around their base. Do not plant them exposed to early morning sun, because rapid thaw can damage the flowers after a frost.

A large tub will take a rhododendron, which should be planted in aicd soil. One cultivar, 'Lee's Scarlet' will bloom at Christmas—others following quickly, *Rhododendron mucronulatum* and *R.* 'Praecox' for instance. There are many species and cultivars of rhododendron which bloom in succession from late autumn to the following late summer.

In autumn early-flowering bulbs should be planted—snowdrops, crocus species and aconites will be the first to bloom, followed later by narcissi and tulips. They can be under-planted in containers of heathers and conifers and will enhance their foliage colours. Many bulbs may be grown in boxes, so you can keep replacing those that have passed their best, providing a constant succession of bright colour.

In the autumn you should look ahead and prepare your containers for colder weather. Clean up all the containers in use. Lift, divide and replant perennials where necessary. A few plants prefer to be moved when the soil is warmer, so leave these till spring. They include delphiniums, michaelmas daisies, kniphofias, scabious and pyrethrums.

When all cleaning up has been completed mulch all plants in containers with peat or some of the leaves that have been falling from the trees, in the last few weeks. If this mulch is likely to be dislodged by winds, anchor it with a layer of pebbles or a piece of chicken wire cut to shape.

LEONARDO FERRANTE

Opposite from Left to Right: *The jungly plants Begonia rex Fan plant Monstera Delicosa, Swiss Cheese or Mexican breadfruit, and Philodendron Scandens, Sweetheart plant.*

Left: *This two floor conservatory has a variety of beautiful pot plants which both look attractive and thrive in this sunny area.*

Above: *A group of architectural contemporary containers suitable for an expensive paved area. They are filled here with a range of colourful spring plants.*
Left: *Terracotta clay pots are available in a wide variety of decorative designs. However do not be afraid to experiment with all kinds of containers for your patio plants. Provided you ensure that any container is properly equipped with drainage holes and is completely in keeping with style of your patio and with other forms of plant holders you already have.*

Index

Handy hints

1. Always ensure that all plans for any project that you undertake are completed, accurately, before you begin.

2. Always check any measurements you will need to take. It will save you time, money and disappointment and ensure a much more professional result if you are extremely careful in the initial stages.

3. Always consult any local by-laws or building restrictions for your area before you invest in tools or materials. It will allow you to incorporate any special features or restrictions that your area may have into your original plans, and avoid expense later.

4. Do take the advice we give about siting, very seriously. It is no use having a beautiful pool or patio that is constantly in the shade, or does not take into account suitable drainage.

5. If you are constructing a permanent pool, do look into the problem of water tables for your area.

6. If you are in any doubt about any aspect of construction, do consult an expert.

7. Do not attempt complex electrical work yourself, remember electricity and water can be a fatal combination.
   Extra precautions should therefore be taken with this aspect of pool construction.